T. E. Davis

From New Jersey to California '97

A History of the Journey of the New Jersey C. E. ...

T. E. Davis

From New Jersey to California '97
A History of the Journey of the New Jersey C. E. ...

ISBN/EAN: 9783744745987

Printed in Europe, USA, Canada, Australia, Japan

Cover: Foto ©Andreas Hilbeck / pixelio.de

More available books at **www.hansebooks.com**

FROM NEW JERSEY
TO CALIFORNIA, '97.

A History of the Journey of the New Jersey
C. E. Special to the Sixteenth International
C. E. Convention, at San Francisco,
July 6--12, 1897.

---

*Compiled by the New Jersey Transportation Manager,
Rev. T. E. Davis, of Bound Brook, N. J.*

PUBLISHED BY C. H. BATEMAN,
EDITOR OF THE UNIONIST-GAZETTE,
SOMERVILLE, N. J.
1897.

Press of
The Unionist-Gazette Association,
Somerville, N. J.

Table of Contents.

	PAGE.
Preface,	5
Preparations for the Great Journey,	7
Sights and Scenes of the Journey,	15
The Scenery.	45
Living By the Way,	49
Sleeping Car Contemplations,	57
The Devotional Meetings,	63
The Convention,	69
San Francisco,	79
Monterey and the Big Trees,	85
Yellowstone Park,	91
New Jersey C. E. Special,	99–138

    Nadura, 100.
    Hebrides, 102.
    Sydenham, 104.
    Superb, 107.
    Saale, 111.
    Alsace, 113.
    Canton, 117.
    Burton, 121.

Utrecht, 125.
Epsom, 127.
Proteus, 131.
Keystone, 135.
Dorante, 137.
New Hampshire, 138.

Hebrides Herald, - - - - - 143
Sydenham Resolutions, - - - - 148

Preface.

Intelligence, or it may be superstition, seems to demand a preface to every book. There may be no more sense in the preface than we made of it in our school-boy days, viz: "Peter Riley Eats Fish And Catches Eels," etc. No one reads a preface, of course. It was not made to be read. It is like the buttons on the sleeves or skirts of a coat, neither useful nor ornamental, but the publisher and critic demand it, and so our preface is here.

We have no apology to offer for this book. It is prepared as a history and souvenir of the wonderful and successful journey of the New Jersey C. E. Special to California, at the request of many of the passengers. We offer it as a memorial of this "trip of a lifetime."

Every year will make this book more valuable. The journey across the continent will be taken each time it is read, and we will live over again and again those happy days. Many of our new made friends will be our friends for life, and not until our eyes behold the land of unfading beauty will we forget the delightful scenes of our own native land.

The journey of the New Jersey Special, including the six days' stay in San Francisco, extended over twenty-six days, and the party travelled over 8,300 miles. We crossed the greatest rivers of our country, visited its largest cities, crossed its most fertile plains and valleys, passed within sight of its highest mountains, and saw its finest fruit orchards and richest grain fields.

One of the party in describing this trip, writes: "I visited twenty-two states, passed through two hundred and fifty cities and towns, crossed seven mountain ranges, went through eighty-seven tunnels, saw twenty-one snow-capped peaks, crossed ninety-one rivers, saw fifty-four lakes, rode on fifteen steamboats, twelve different railroads, and over one hundred street car lines, saw forty-seven waterfalls, three snow storms, three glaciers, thirty-five geysers, five thousand hot springs, received ten thousand kindnesses, and only one unkind word, etc."

The record of such a trip should be held in "everlasting remembrance."

The thanks of all those who were on the New Jersey C. E. Special are due to the generous contributors who furnished the articles for this book. We add a list of such names as far as known:

Rev. L. R. Dyott,
  F. C. Ottman,
  J. B. Kugler,
  A. P. Peake,
  A. I. Martine,
  D. R. Warne,
  A. A. Murphy,
  W. E. Davis,
  W. T. S. Lumbar,
  T. E. Davis,

Mr. N. Y. Dungan,
  H. H. Wainwright,
  W. F. Overman,
  C. H. Bateman,
  F. A. Foster,
Miss Mary F. Van Alen,
  Rose M. Egbert,
  H. Estelle Roe,
  Jennie A. Wrigley,
  R. Anna Miller,

    Miss Margaret J. Wade.

Preparations for the Great Journey.

And now it came to pass when the Christian Endeavorers had become mighty in the land, even an exceeding great army, that the chief rulers said we will hold a grand convocation in the city, which is on the borders of the great western sea. And so this decree was issued and noised abroad throughout all the land and across the sea, even to the uttermost parts of the earth: Behold the Sixteenth Annual Convention draweth nigh. On the seventh day of the seventh month, all good Endeavorers who have talents of gold and talents of silver will meet together in the great temple called the Mechanic's Pavilion, which is in the city of San Francisco.

Now in those days Clement, who was of the house of French, a man of goodly countenance and of high repute, was the chief ruler of the Endeavorers in the land which is called New Jersey.

Now when Clement had called all his chief officers and captains together in the great city, which is Trenton, he said, men and brethren, behold tidings have come to me of a mighty gathering of our people in the far-away land of California. And it has further come to my ears that many of our young men and maidens, likewise old men and lone widows are going thither.

Now it is not good that maidens and widows should be alone.

And I have heard also there are many dangers by the way, also robbers and beasts of prey that may injure or molest our unprotected daughters and sisters. Let us, therefore, select one of our number, a man discreet and valorous, who shall conduct our people safely to the great assembly and bring them hither in peace.

And the thing seemed good to all those who were in authority.

And Clement said, whom shall we select and who shall our chosen leader be?

And a certain beardless young man whose surname was Mason, said, there is one in our midst who has had experience in such matters. Titus, who sojourns on the great river, that is the Raritan, and now if it seems good to all who are present, I move that we cast our lots for him as our Transportation Manager.

And the thing seemed good to all the chief officers and captains and they all cast lots for Titus.

Now when Titus was chosen to lead the Endeavorers from New Jersey to the land which is nigh unto the Golden Gate, he said, behold now it is a mighty work and I fear lest the burden be too heavy for one alone to bear.

So I will choose other men, and they shall be men of wisdom and of great courage and of exceeding great patience, for the journey is long and there will be many evil and troublesome people who will greatly harass and vex us. So he appointed William, who dwelt among the cedars of Lebanon, and Elias, upon whom the mantle of Nathaniel had fallen.

He also selected Sherman for the long march across the country, and Ruby of the tribe of Dan.

But these were all men of peace. None of them were accustomed to the sound of war.

NEW JERSEY TO CALIFORNIA, '97.

Therefore, Titus said, peradventure, we may meet giants in the land whither they go. These men may be fearful and flee when no man pursueth. I will, therefore, select a man who shall be a terror to every foe that we may meet in the wild country through which we journey. And so Abram the Great, he of the mighty stature and fearful mien was chosen. For it is still well known how on the foot ball fields of Princeton, Yale and Columbia he had been victorious over many a mighty foe. Now these are the men who were to lead the Endeavorers to the Convention by the great western sea, but Titus was chief.

Now when the days were near at hand that the journey should begin Titus said, behold there are many of the aged who will go with us, likewise there are many young and tender maidens. Now the distance is too great for them to journey on foot; nor can Abram and the other mighty men carry them all the way over the high mountains and through the deep rivers.

And so it was that Titus said to Samuel, who was of the house of Wilson, the same was the faithful servant of George, who dwelt in the town of Pullman, behold now I have a great host of people who will go with me to the great assembly in the land of gold, and I have heard that George, thy master, is well able to transport all of our people, so that none of them need to go on foot. Now I beseech thee send this message to thy master.

Thy servants, the Endeavorers, which dwell in the land of mosquitos, otherwise called New Jersey, desire some of the finest carriages to convey them to the great meeting.

And George answered Samuel. It is well. Behold it hath already been told me that our brethren in New Jersey are of good understanding and honorable character, Now thus shall ye do and more also unto them. The very finest of the cars that are in the region round about Gotham shall be given to the brethren from New Jersey, and in these shall they go on their long journey, and in these shall they return. And if any shall say unto thee, why showest thou these favors unto the Endeavorers from New Jersey, thou shalt answer, these are the people whom George delighteth to honor.

Now when Titus had communicated with all those who were in authority in his own country, he found that many could not go. One had married a wife and domestic duties and responsibilities were too great. Another was hoping to be married soon, and, therefore, could not go now. Others had urgent business that hindered their going, and still others whose shekels had not multiplied sufficiently, could not go. Two of the great men, Clement and Cornelius said, wherefore now should we cross this vast country again. We have journeyed once over its plains and mountains, and it is not needful that we go now, for Luther who is also a chief officer and a mighty captain, and withal an honorable man, will go with you, so while Titus leads and Abram terrifies the foe, Luther will provide a rich diet to feed upon. So of all the chief men and women in this goodly land of New Jersey, only five did go to the great convention, Luther and Titus, with William the good physician, and the other William the good citizen, and Elias the sweet singer from the great falls.

And now when the thing began to be noised abroad, there was a great tumult in all the province, and the people began to write to Titus to ask about the trip and the wondrous things they would see, and the price thereof. And they sent so many Epistles that the number thereof was three score and ten each day. And many could not wait to write, but came in haste to the town where Titus dwelt; even a great crowd so that he could scarcely eat or sleep for waiting on them. And when the number multiplied exceedingly, Titus said, the people who are to go with me are already a great host, and I cannot take any more, for I cannot give them food to eat, nor can I find lodging places for them, neither can I bring them to the Convention in time. But the crowd besought him the more eagerly, saying, we must go with thee, and we will lodge upon the floor of the car; and others said, when we come to the desert we will feed on the sand which is there. And because of their vehemence of speech, and because they troubled him, Titus said, I will secure other cars and there shall be a second train and you shall go. Howbeit when trouble or delay or hunger comes, know ye that all things have come to pass because of the vast multitude, and ye must not murmur or complain. And they said, we will not murmur or complain.

Nevertheless, many of them forgot all their good promises, and ceased not to grumble, except for the few hours when sleep closed their mouths, and there was peace.

And now it came to pass when four hundred and two score and ten were numbered among those who were to go to the great Convention, that Titus said, I will not take any more. And so the number of those who were turned away was an hundred and thirty and six. Nevertheless on the day when the host departed there were some who said, we have loved ones who are going, and we must go with them, and others climbed up some other way into the cars, and were not found until far on the journey.

And behold when they were numbered it was found there were four hundred and four score and one souls in the great company. And the hearts of Titus and the chief captains with him waxed sore, and they said, what shall we do with all these people, and where shall they lodge.

But when the night was fully come, a lodging place had been found for every man and woman, so that only one had to recline upon the floor.

Now among this mighty host there were many good and honorable men and youth, likewise women and maidens. So that as they journeyed the people in the towns whither they came were greatly astonished and said, we have seen many trains from the East, but none which held so many wise men and such fair women. Truly these are the fairest and best of the sons of men. And when it was told them that all these were Endeavorers from the goodly land of New Jersey, they were the more astonished, and said, since they have brought all their people with them, wherefore did they not also carry their country along.

Now in the great multitude that journeyed westward, there were one and twenty High Priests, beside one tender youth who was preparing for the same office. And these men all did good service in ministering to the spiritual wants of the people, and warning the unruly and wayward ones.

But these men could not relieve the aching body and drive away pain, and so it was deemed prudent to take along skillful men and women, who should act as physicians to Ward off disease, and who would not be Slack in answering the calls of the needy and suffering when they might Howl with pain. And so eight of the wisest and best of all the physicians in New Jersey were taken along. And these men and women did noble service and were held in high esteem by all the people.

There came also other great men who were renowned as doctors of the law, and whose fame had already spread far and wide. Among them was Nelson, also a great musical author. Bloomfield the Littel, and Halstead the great historian.

These men also rendered great service so that no one of this great multitude from New Jersey were put in prison or hanged during the journey.

And the number of those who were given to the training of the youth far exceeded those of any other occupation. So that the teachers alone were more than a hundred who went from New Jersey to the great Convention.

And now when all things were ready, and when each one had paid their fare, the great trains began to move, and the long journey was begun.

But the great things that happened by the way, and the wonderful things that were seen, behold now are not these all written in the chronicles of the wise men and women that follow.

Sights and Scenes of the Journey.

On Monday morning, June 28, 1897, at nine o'clock, the New Jersey Endeavorers and their friends started on their long journey across the continent, to attend the Sixteenth International Convention of the C. E. Society at San Francisco. Fourteen Pullman palace cars were required to carry the large party. These made a train so large that it was necessary to divide it into two sections, one of which was in charge of the Transportation Manager, Rev. T. E. Davis, and the other under the care of one of his assistants, Rev. A. I. Martine.

Short stops were made to take on passengers at Elizabethport, Elizabeth, Plainfield, Bound Brook, Trenton and Philadelphia. After leaving the last city, the passengers felt that the long journey had really begun, and began to look around and acquaint themselves with those who were to be their companions for that ride of over eight thousand miles. Many new friendships were thus formed that will never fade until time itself shall end.

The first day's ride was through the states of New Jersey, Pennsylvania, Delaware and Maryland. It is indeed a picturesque country through which the Baltimore and Ohio trains pass, but the scenery is not to be compared with the magnificent sights that awaited us farther on. A short stop at Harper's Ferry was allowed the first section, but only long enough to gain a glimpse of the beautiful Potomac River as it breaks through the Alleghany Mountains.

The monument which marks the place made famous by John Brown, was the only object of historic interest seen. During the night the Appallachian Mountains were crossed, and when the Endeavorers awoke on Tuesday morning, they found no scenery which even approached that of New Jersey. There were only the flat, marshy fields and stunted woods of Southern Indiana and Illinois during all that day, and many a heart felt a growing pride in Jersey, as compared with what they saw of these states.

At Cincinnati a good breakfast was served at the Grand Hotel, on Tuesday morning, but there was no time to look at this Ohioan city. We took dinner at Vincennes, and arrived at St. Louis about two hours late. At least this is the story of the first section which reached this western end of the Baltimore and Ohio. The second section was four hours late, and having been that late for their dinners at Vincennes, they were not in a very agreeable humor when they came up with their comrades for the first time since the start from New York. The atmosphere in the magnificent depot in St. Louis was stifling—aye, it fairly sizzled the journeying Endeavorers from more northern latitudes. A few went to the Planter's Hotel and delighted themselves inspecting the Turkish rooms and the other beautiful appointments, but the city was dark and forbidding, and with melted collars and streaming brows the travellers soon returned to the trains, and endeavored to fan themselves into coolness, while they waited impatiently for the orders of the despatchers to start the trains. But all things end in this world, and about mid-night the first section pulled out of the St. Louis station, closely followed by the second division.

From St. Louis to Kansas City the state was traversed at night, but the latter city was reached three hours late, and during the whole trip the heat was intense. Sleep was scarcely possible, and it was a tired and hungry lot of Endeavorers who alighted for breakfast at ten o'clock on Wednesday. There they found plenty of the same kind of Endeavorers waiting for their trains to go out. The heat in the train yards was almost unbearable, but the travellers remained there for three hours, while the man who despatched the trains sat coolly locked in his tower, and refused to give out any information to the sweltering crowds. When the trains finally moved out towards the western plains, there were no regrets left behind for Kansas City.

The trip across Kansas was enjoyed more than that of any other state previously crossed. The scenery along the Rock Island road is very picturesque. The growing crops and trees look beautiful this year. The big corn fields promise a tremendous yield, and acres upon acres of potatoes stretch along the railroad. The thrifty, well-kept farms, and the neat farm houses and buildings are in marked contrast with those of Indiana and Ohio. When the prairies were reached in western Kansas, there were many interesting things to attract the eastern eye. The small homes of the farmers, the strange looking villages with one-story houses, the prairie dogs, the abandoned sod houses the big canvas covered wagons and many other objects took up their attention. The intense heat had been followed by cool breezes, and altogether it was a pleasant time.

But it was to Colorado that all eyes were looking forward with eager expectation. Early on the morning of July 1, the boundary line between Kansas and Colorado was crossed, and the Rocky Mountains became visible, but it was two in the afternoon when the last section approached the Manitou station. As two o'clock the following morning was the hour fixed for leaving, there were many disappointed cries from those who had anticipated so much from their stay in this magnificent spot. When the two locomotives, which were pulling the train up the steep grade, were stalled when half way up the last hill, the impatience broke out with a vehemence. But we were finally deposited at the little station almost at the base of Pike's Peak, and during the lunch at the Manitou House, every one's spirits were aroused by the announcement that the time of staying would be extended until two o'clock the next afternoon. Every New Jersey Endeavorer hurried with his or her lunch, and every moment of the time was occupied with drives through the Garden of the gods, and the various canons famed throughout the world for their picturesque beauty, or in ascending Pike's Peak, whose rugged brow frowned upon the lesser heights below.

The Garden of the gods, how strange! Nature was in a weird mood when she formed these rocks. Entering from the Manitou side we pass Balance Rock, a huge mass which has so slender a foundation as to make one feel that it is about to fall over. On one side stands a statue of liberty leaning on her shield, with the conventional Phrygian cap on her head; there is a gigantic frog, a turtle, a lion, all carved in sandstone; yonder is a pilgrim, staff in hand; just a little further is the plain figure of a woman; there are a seal and the large figure of an elephant. These all stand out so clearly that it would seem some Titan hand had carved these shapes. In some instances the figures are of red sandstone, and the pedestals are of contrasting hue. It would not take a lively imagination to discover in this

Garden an endless variety of imitative forms of human beings, of birds and beasts and reptiles. They stand on the hillsides above and around us. They are right by our wagon wheels. They seem to be real living beings, with whom we would fain be acquainted, but for whom we have too much veneration. Now we ascend to the top of a hill and a panorama of surpassing grandeur is about us. Behind rises Pike's Peak, bare, forbidding, grand, with her fellows, clad in deep green, cowering close to her skirts. Before, we see the grandest formations of the Garden— the great rocks forming a natural gateway to it. Two lofty tablets of carnelian-colored sandstone, set directly opposite each other, about fifty feet apart, and rising to a height of three hundred and thirty feet, form the portals of this far-famed gateway. On the top of one of these rocks is the distinct figure of a lamb, while the top of the other is shaped into the form of a huge lion. Surely if this is the work of nature, the lion and the lamb have been made to lie down together. Just to the right of the gateway are the cathedral spires, which are of a similar character to the gateway, but their crests are sharply splintered into spire-like pinnacles.

The brilliant carnelian hue of these sandstones, outlined against the deep blue sky, and gilded by the light of a Colorado sun, cannot be described. We passed out of the Gardens through these wonderful portals with the same feeling that one would have in emerging from one of the great English cathedrals.

Some of the New Jersey party who arrived on the first section earlier in the day, ascended Pike's Peak the same afternoon, but for the others, through the persistent efforts of several members of the party, a special sunrise trip was arranged by the Cog Wheel Railway. It was with some discomfort that we arose at two o'clock in the morning and started for the railway station, and it was still more annoying to be obliged to wait at the station for two hours for the train to steam up, but we were on our way to the summit ere the first streaks of dawn appeared over the peaks. Pike's Peak is not the highest one in Colorado. There are twenty others which rise from a few feet to three hundred feet higher, but Pike's Peak is the most accessible. Formerly its top could only be reached by bold climbers, or on the backs of burros, but now the trip can be made in an hour by the cog railway. Every eastern traveler is disappointed at the height of the peak, which is 14,147 feet above sea level, but this is due to a comparison with eastern mountains, without a consideration of the surrounding height. The town of Manitou is 6,324 feet above sea level, which is about the height of Mount Washington in New Hampshire. Just outside of Colorado Springs we were shown a small hill about two hundred feet high, called Mount Washington, because its height is just that of the mountain which so many tourists ascend in the East. Starting from a base which was on a line with the top of Mount Washington, Pike's Peak towers eight thousand feet above. Huge banks of snow could be seen glistening in the sun light during the day previous, while it was quite warm at Manitou.

The cars are not drawn up by cables, but are pushed by a locomotive in the rear. In some places the grades are startling, but the curious engines seem to have no trouble in pushing steadily upward. It is eight miles from the starting point to the summit. Thick woods of hemlock, oak and fir trees are on either side as we gradually ascend. Huge masses of rocks are piled up to the height of a thousand feet, one big boulder hanging to another in the wildest profusion, as though they had been thrown there by some great upheaval of nature. Beautiful ravines we pass through, down which tumble mountain streams, with an occasional waterfall leaping many feet from rock to rock. Nature begins to exhibit her most stern characteristics. As we get above the tops of the smaller peaks, a splendid panorama presents itself. The sky is without clouds, except near the horizon. The sun is yet hidden behind the peaks, but is stretching up her rosy arms towards the zenith. Now we are at timber line. Above us rise the bare rocks and loose sand, which form the barren summit of the mountain we are ascending. Not a twig to be seen, but a few patches of snow to relieve the gray. Below us the beautiful green foliage, the mountain flowers in such marked contrast to the barrenness about us. Away out on the vistas beyond, to the south, to the east, such a glorious view of mountain ranges in successive heights, outlined against the sky, most of them clad in their foliage of green, but some of the higher peaks capped with snow.

The first rays of the sun are now touching these peaks, and as each of them are lighted up, the effect is beyond the pen to describe. One hundred and twenty-five miles away the eye can see these magnificent mountains, whose snow caps are painted in so many different colors by the king of the morning, who has now aroused himself to his daily task. It is a glorious sight which must impress one with its grandeur so long as the mind's eye can see.

As we approach the summit, the atmosphere gets very cold, and the warmest wraps do not feel amiss. There are huge banks of snow on either side of the track, and we seem to have been suddenly transported to some frigid clime. The grade is very steep here, and the timid shrink from looking down the way we have come. Round and round the peak we go, higher and higher, until at last with a loud snort the hump-backed locomotive gives us a final push right up on the top, and beyond where any other railroad reaches. We alight and then drink in the glorious view of nature's grandest works, with a clear atmosphere and the sun still adding his touches as he ascends the heavens. It is a sight not soon to be forgotten. The summit is not of large extent, and the party wandered about on the snow and ice, gathering souvenirs, shivering with cold and forgetful that it was July 2, and a sweltering day at home. Several were severely affected by the high altitude, and were obliged to keep quiet during their stay on the summit.

The descent was noteworthy, only in a repetition of the views already described, and it was a hungry party which arrived at the Manitou House about an hour later for breakfast.

Pike's Peak is only one of the glories of Manitou. Few places have so many. Surrounded by sublimities, the visitor may stay a long time without being at a loss for a new canon or mountain stream or other point of interest. They abound in every direction. The members of the New Jersey Special scattered through the mountains, and at most of the points of interest could be seen the orange and black badge of the Christian Endeavorers. We visited Cheyenne canon, some distance from Colorado Springs, and it proved a most delightful trip. The rocky walls of the canon rise 2,000 feet straight above the roadway, which winds along a beautiful stream. The falls at the head of the canon are very beautiful. This was the favorite resort of Helen Hunt Jackson, and we were pointed to the lone peak upon which her remains were interred at her request. They have since been removed to Colorado City. We rode about Colorado Springs, which has some splendid residences, and is said to be the wealthiest city of its size in the United States, though its population is but 2,500. Many mine owners live here.

Leaving Manitou on the afternoon of July 3, the New Jersey Special started on its way across the Rocky Mountains. We reached the Grand Canon of the Arkansas just before sunset, and passed through this magnificent gorge, just when the finest shadow effects were upon the cliffs. It was a ride which gives one a lasting impression. The train moves slowly along the bank of the river, with the rocks overhanging in some places. At times one end of the train is hidden behind the cliffs as the track curves sharply around the base of a huge rock. The great rocky walls are shaped into all sorts of domes and pinnacles up where they seem to meet the sky. Sometimes they slant backward like a man who tries to walk too straight. Then they lean forward and seem about to topple over into the river below. Again they stand out alone, slender and graceful. The river tumbles down among the rocks in a ruby torrent, but its music adds to the sublimity of the occasion. The two locomotives pant wearily as they drag the long, heavy train around the sharp curves. The coaches creak and groan, and the echoes of the rumbling train reverberate through the arches of the canon. The crested crags grow higher as we advance into the heart of the mountains, and the river seems to foam more madly. The way becomes a mere fissure through the heights over which the sky forms a gray arch in the twilight. The place is a measureless gulf of air with solid walls on either side. Here the granite cliffs are a thousand feet high, smooth and unbroken by tree or shrub; there a pinnacle soars skyward for thrice that distance. No flowers are to be seen, nor are any birds visible. Nothing but impenetrable solitude. The grandest portion of the canon is reached, where a long iron bridge hangs suspended from the smooth walls of the cliffs. Truly man has triumphed over nature here. When first examined it seemed impossible that a railway could be constructed through this canon. There was scarcely room for the river alone, and granite ledges blocked the path with their mighty bulk. But the obstructions were blasted away, and a road bed was made closely following the detour of the cliffs. The river is not over twenty feet wide in many places, so that one can well imagine how profound is this gorge through the mountains, when we consider its great depth.

Emerging from the gorge, the narrow valley of the Arkansas was traversed, beautiful indeed, the striking serrated peaks of the Sangre de Cristo range close at hand on the west, until Salida was reached, where the New Jersey party spent the night in their cars awaiting daylight to continue their journey across this great range of mountains.

Salida is a prosperous mountain town of 3,500 population. It has an altitude of seven thousand and fifty feet. It is the junction of the standard gauge main line leading via Leadville, Tennessee Pass and Glenwood Springs to Grand Junction, and the narrow gauge line, via Marshall Pass to another connection with the main line at Grand Junction. The party divided at this place, the larger portion taking cars on the narrow gauge to cross the world-famed Marshall Pass, while the remainder in our own coaches went around the other way. Both routes are unrivalled for their magnificent mountain scenery and for engineering skill displayed in constructing railroad tracks up the steep mountain sides. The Marshall Pass route is generally considered more wonderful of the two by travelers. Leaving Salida early in the morning, we began the steep ascent to the top of the Pass, which is 10,852 feet above the sea level. The track winds up the mountains in great loops, each one a little higher than the other, until when the summit is reached, one can look down upon four lines of track, terrace beyond terrace, the last so far below as to be indistinct to view. At times the train slowly rounds sharp curves, where the passenger can look far down into valleys, thousands of feet below making him hold his breath as he gazes into the dizzy depths, and he wonders how the train ever gained those heights, even with two locomotives tugging away at it.

But, oh, the surpassing grandeur of the scenery! As the train progressed up the steep grade, the view became less obstructed by mountain sides, and the eye roamed over miles of cone-shaped summits. But exceeding all else in grandeur were the snow-shrouded peaks of the Sangre de Cristo range. Those near at hand are clearly defined, and then the range extends to the southward until cloud and sky and snowy peak commingle and form a vague and bewildering vision. The most beautiful peak of all as seen from the high altitude on Mount Ouray, was Mount Antero of the Sagnache range, which was nearer by, and was so enveloped with snow far down its slopes that it seemed to be wrapped in a great sheet.

Mount Ouray holds the pass, and towers grand, solitary and forbidding to our right. And now while we are in raptures over the snow-capped peaks in the distance, the snow begins to fall about us. First it came lightly, and then developed into a real storm as we continued to ascend. The hemlock and fir trees caught it in their branches, and soon were as white as in a mid-winter storm. The ground was nearly covered, and yet the beautiful flowers peeped through and added color to the scene. The whole party was so charmed by the novelty and beauty of the storm, that when the train pulled into the sheds at the summit they rushed from the cars pell-mell and began snow balling each other furiously. The snow was two or three inches in depth, and it was an event of a life time for Jerseymen to snow-ball each other on the Fourth of July. In the midst of it all, some one began singing the long metre doxology, and the entire party joined in heartily. It was an impressive moment.

The descent to Gunnison was very beautiful, but not so thrilling as the ascent. The view through the deep ravines was magnificent. We took dinner at Gunnison, a flourishing town, 7,680 feet above sea level. Here we tasted the far-famed trout of the Gunnison. Then followed a ride through the famous black canon of the Gunnison river. Here again the railroad lies for many miles upon a shelf hewn from the living rock which frequently rises to an altitude of over 2,000 feet. The river is even more beautiful than the Arkansas as it foams madly over its rocky bottom. The great cliffs almost meet overhead at times, and the huge rocks are piled up into fantastic shapes. For sixteen miles the route lies through this magnificent canon, which rivals the canon of the Arkansas and the Royal Gorge in grandeur.

Emerging from the canon we had a splendid view of the Ouray Mountains, with Mount Sneffles rising more than 14,000 feet towards the heavens. They were completely enveloped in snow, and with the brilliant touches of the afternoon sun, they had the appearance of crystal mountains. Some who had seen the mountains of Switzerland, declared that these came nearer to them in beauty than any they had seen. For miles this range was in view, and we left it behind with reluctance.

We reached Grand Junction in the early evening, but our train, which came over the Tennessee Pass, did not arrive until eleven. The party on board were equally enthusiastic over their ride, which had been very picturesque and grand.

Grand Junction is about the only place in Colorado that the Christian Endeavorers left without regret. Especially was this true of those who had spent the day on the narrow gauge road without the comforts of their own easy coaches, and who were forced to roam about an uninteresting town where good food was at a premium, awaiting the arrival of their train. Many trains arrived at Grand Junction that evening, and those were fortunate who could get a palatable supper. Just on the verge of the Egyptian desert we were advised to get provision for the future, and there was a general foraging of the town. A woman who had driven in from the country with a can of milk, which she sold in huge black bottles, did quite a thriving business by the wayside, but the sight of tender maidens wearing the C. E. badge trudging along with those black bottles was rather amusing.

The Grand Valley comprises several counties, and is said to have a soil of remarkable richness, upon which every kind of agricultural product flourishes luxuriantly. As it was dark when we started out from Grand Junction, we saw little of this section, and when we awakened the following morning we were in the midst of the Egyptian desert, which is a part of the Great American desert. Nothing but sage brush could be seen in the way of vegetation, but the most wonderful formations attracted our attention. On the north, for a long time, were the richly colored Book-cliffs. To the south could be seen the snow-clad summits of the Sierra la Sal, and San Rafel, glistening in the distance. All along the way the foot of hills and cliffs had the most fantastic shapes that almost rivalled the Garden of the gods. Here the top of the cliff had the appearance of a huge Egyptian temple with its low roofs, eaves adorned with fancy stone sculptured from the rocks, and windows in their proper places. There were pinnacles and obelisks and sphinxes and great crumbling ruins. They were colored sufficiently to suit the most vivid imagination. Some times they were red and some times grey. Some times the walls were straight and well preserved, and at other times they were falling down. The cliffs would have a half dozen different colored strata in some places, and looked as though swift water had cut them asunder, and washed up against them, first one way and then another.

When Sunday morning dawned, we had been due in Salt Lake City since mid-night of Saturday. The managers were cross at being obliged to travel on the Sabbath, and some of the party were indignant, but we were in the hands of the railroads, and patience seemed the most important virtue. We passed through a few small settlements where the inhabitants lived in miserable huts, but not until we reached Helper, where the ascent of the Wasatch Mountains began, did we have another opportunity to forage for provisions. While the train was supplied with ice and water, those who were fortunate enough to own a tin pail or a bottle, hurried to the little wooden stores, just back of the station, forgetful in their hunger, it was the Sabbath day. All the milk and bread and sandwiches were soon cleaned up in that town, and the rest of the time was occupied in talking to the natives, most of whom work for the railroad company. A service of song was held at the station, which attracted many of them.

Helper and Castle Gate, which is only a mile distant, are surrounded by high cliffs of startling beauty, similar to those already described, only higher and grander. Most of the natives are Mormons, and there were a number of snap shots taken of the little Mormon children, who looked curiously at our trains. At Castle Gate were large coke ovens and mining operations are in progress in the mountains. At the entrance to Castle Canon stand two towering sand stone shafts, which rise to a height of 500 feet, looking like two monstrous castles, with battlements, bastions and turrets guarding the way, and just wide enough apart to allow the train to pass between. The canon which follows is another of sublime beauty. Castle Gate is so called because of two huge pillars or ledges of rock, which tower to a great height, with the river dashing down between. The railroad has forced a passage by its side between these two sharp promontories.

Following up this grand gorge, the train makes its way into the heart of the Wasatch Mountains, reaching Soldier Summit at an elevation of 7,465 feet. Passing through the Red Narrows and Spanish Fork Canon, we entered the beautiful Utah Valley, and realized the joy of the Mormons, when, weary with long travel in their lumbering wagons over the desert, they saw this picturesque valley before them with Utah Lake, a beautiful sheet of clear, fresh water in the midst.

All the way from this point to Salt Lake City the scenery was charming. The Wasatch Mountains, perfectly void of foliage, have a strange appearance after the Rockies. From a distance they look like huge elephants with blue skins. The valley is like a well-kept garden, and is a delightful relief from the barren desert. Farm joins farm, and all are so well irrigated that the crops look luxuriant, and fruit trees are in rich profusion. Neat homes are on every side, and the whole country looks thrifty.

The shadows of evening were getting long when the train drew into Salt Lake City, where we were to remain until the next day. That evening a large mass meeting was held in the big Mormon Tabernacle, and most of the New Jersey Endeavorers were present. The Tabernacle was thrown open for the occasion, and some of the Mormon elders spoke, as well as Christian Endeavorers. This great building, which seats about 10,000 people, and is only surpassed for seating capacity by the Ocean Grove Auditorium in this country, was decorated with the national colors, and a large C. E. badge had been placed on the big organ, the largest organ in this country, and only surpassed by one other in the world. The exercises were exceedingly interesting, and the worshipers felt a strange thrill to have participated in a service in a temple, which was formerly not a welcome place to gentiles.

Salt Lake City is really an attractive place to an Eastern visitor, more because of its associations than its beauty as a city. To compare it with cities of same population in the East, would place it in a high rank. Yet it has beautiful wide avenues, splendid shade trees, some magnificent buildings, and first class street railway service. Great Salt Lake is a beautiful body of water, of which any city might well be proud, and many were the New Jersey men and maidens who enjoyed a dip in its saline waters, and the fresh water shower bath which follows. Saltaire is the great resort for the city, and a handsome pavilion is erected there for bathers. The handsome State Capitol is also well worth a visit, from the top of which there is a splendid view of the surrounding country.

But the places with which Mormonism is associated, are the centre of attraction here. The Tabernacle and Temple are beautifully located in one large square, surrounded by a high stone wall. The Tabernacle is not an attractive building from the exterior, but is low, with a rounding roof. The lower portion is built of homely brick. Its seating capacity and its large organ are the only redeeming features. Here is where the Mormons have their great gatherings. But the Temple is a magnificent structure which cost about $4,000,000. No gentile can enter this and Mormons only have admission as they desire to be baptized or married. The interior appointments are said to be very handsome. The work on the Temple was largely done by the Mormon mechanics, who gave a certain portion of their time, rather than cash subscriptions. The gold figure of the patron angel of the Mormons, adorns the topmost pinnacle, blowing a trumpet.

It was with interest that we visited the Tithing house, where all the church moneys are sent, and from which they are distributed for various benevolent purposes; the "Bee Hive," where Brigham Young resided for a long time with his numerous wives; the present home of his surviving favorite wife, and finally the quiet little plot where are buried many of his wives.

Salt Lake City filled the whole party with curiosity to see her peculiar institutions. All came away convinced that Mormonism is not on the decline, while its offensive features may not be so prominent as before.

The ride from Salt Lake City to the foot of the Sierra Nevada Mountains, is across the Alkali plains, which compose the most arid portion of the Great American desert. It is a day's ride over this barren waste, where there is no vegetation but the sage brush, which seems to maintain a sort of existence despite the lack of moisture. Sometimes this trip is fraught with very much discomfort, owing to the dust which blows over the trains in such clouds that all the windows of the cars have to be kept tightly closed in order to have any degree of comfort. Fortunately for the New Jersey party the weather was auspicious, the atmosphere was cool and there was little dust. Had it been otherwise, the Jerseymen, accustomed though they are to sand dunes, would have been a woe-begone lot when they reached California. For owing to the delays incident upon a large number of special trains, it took two days and a night to span the desert. The trip was not without interest, however. There were little hamlets at long intervals, where inhabitants lived in dugouts, or in mere shanties. How they could be content in such a monotonous dreariness, was a mystery which the Endeavorers could not solve. Some of them were in the employ of the railroad company, and others had ranches on the neighboring hills, where they had large herds of cattle grazing. From the train these hillsides seemed as barren as the plains, but the natives said there were excellent pasture lands in some of the ravines. At one place a Boston woman was found as mistress of an humble abode, and she was delighted to talk with people from the East, which she had left many years ago.

At Terrace, an humble hamlet with nothing but sand dunes, and the distant mountains surrounding it, there was a stop for such food as could be obtained at the close of the first day out. Most of the party had provided for this desert trip, and ate their meals in the cars with the best grace possible. Some had provided themselves with oil or alcohol stoves, and had a regular culinary establishment in their sections. But others were glad to get a cup of coffee, or some daintily cooked food, when the opportunity came.

Two ministers occupied a stateroom in the Superb. They had a cooking outfit, and were quite a success in operating it. But at Terrace they entered an old colored woman's hut and asked for something to eat. Old aunty was so confused at the crowd of strangers that she was unable to perform her duties, and made slow progress for the hungry dominies. So one of them seized the skillet from her hands and the other took the eggs and broke them into the pan, and between them they prepared a palatable meal for which they paid liberally. About the same hour that they were doing this humble work, one of the ministers was on the program of the great convention to make an address, but there they were stalled in the great desert.

There were many amusing incidents of that ride across the plains. There were frequent stops, and the weary travellers would get off and wander about. They entered the cabins of the natives, when they could, plied them with all sorts of questions, and must have convinced those denizens of the desert that curiosity was not the exclusive faculty of woman. Religious meetings were held in the cars every day, and frequently there would be a song service on the station platform, while the natives gathered around. At Wadsworth there was an old woman who listened to the singing with tears in her eyes. She said she had walked a long distance to hear these gospel hymns, which she had not listened to for 30 years.

It was at Wadsworth, too, that a pleasant incident happened. Rev. T. E. Davis, the transportation manager, was called to the station platform while the train waited, and was presented with a purse of $115 by Rev. Dr. Chapman. This had been contributed by the Endeavorers as a token of their regard for his work. Mr. Simmons, the Pullman conductor, was also presented with a purse of $36.

At Reno, we stopped for supper the second day, Wednesday. It was a rough and tumble Western town, but it had so many characteristics of a live civilization that everybody rejoiced. The desert was crossed, and before dark we entered the beautiful scenery of the Sierra Nevada Mountains. Then followed the 40 miles of snow sheds, and when we emerged it was too dark to see more. When we awoke the following morning, we were almost to Oakland, which bears the same relation to San Francisco that Jersey City does to New York. We had passed through Sacramento during the night, and those who were awake saw a magnificent station brilliantly lighted with electric globes, which spelled the word "Welcome." The C. E. Committee had been waiting for many hours to receive the New Jersey party, but found few of them awake. The train crossed the Sacramento river, on what is reputed to be the largest ferry boat in the world. The train was divided into two sections, but the whole train was on the boat at one time.

California, the end of the long journey across the continent, the Mecca of the C. E. hosts, is a wonderful State. We saw it at a disadvantage, doubtless, as it was the dry season. The foliage looked thirsty and weary of life, and while the flowers and the fields and the orchards were objects of wonder to us Jerseymen, yet they were somewhat disappointing, for the reason just mentioned.

We caught the first side glimpse of the Golden Gate as we crossed the bay, a three mile ride from Oakland, but its glories were to be better appreciated later. The bay is a beautiful sheet of water, when the sun is shining upon its bosom.

Everyone gazed upon San Francisco with curious eyes. Much was expected of this great city, which has had such a romantic history. One could not help but look upon its beautiful buildings and recall the fact that but few years had passed since the same ground was only covered by tents which protected the gold hunters who crowded thither from all parts of the world to seek their fortunes.

San Francisco is a city of hills. The grades up which the cable cars climb, almost make your hair stand when you look below. Yet the whole city is interwoven with the finest system of cable roads that we came across. One can ride to the extreme end of the city and get several transfers to different sections for a single fare. Up and down these streets they go, never changing their speed, at an angle which prohibits the use of other vehicles in many places. The Golden Gate Park, the Cliff House and Sutro Heights, Chinatown and the Presidio, the government reservation, were the most prominent places of resort, and they would be a credit to any city. Golden Gate Park is beautifully located with Strawberry Hill in the centre, rising far above the rest, and from the top of which there is a magnificent view of the Pacific and the Golden Gate. The Cliff House is built on the rocks which jut out into the ocean about fifty feet from the surface. A hundred feet away are the seal rocks, upon which the sea lions bask in the sun every day. From the hotel far around to the north, stretches the rocky coast, the only break being the entrance to the Golden Gate. It is a picturesque spot. Most of the party walked down to the sands below the hotel, where the beach looks more like our own New Jersey, and dipped their hands of the western ocean. Many of them enjoyed the Sutro baths, which are said to be the finest in the world. The

Sutro Gardens are filled with tropical vegetation of the most luxuriant kind.

Mechanic's Pavilion was where the convention was held. A portion of the building was devoted to bureaus of information for each of the States. Any information desired could be obtained here about the meetings, or about the city, or any of the side excursions. Yet there was seating capacity in the audience room for nearly 10,000 persons. It was a wonderful sight to witness these great audiences of enthusiastic people, and this was especially true when they gave the handkerchief salute. It was estimated that 40,000 Christian Endeavorers were gathered in the city, and of course they made a big crowd when they came together. There were other halls where overflow meetings were held, and all of the churches were open. Everything was given up to C. E. The stores were decorated with the colors, the streets were bright with streamers and flags with C. E. emblems, and at night a huge arch of electric lights over Market street, reminded the thousands who must pass beneath that the Christian Endeavorers were in town. Yet the halls were all so well managed that those who were fortunate enough to get inside were not in the least inconvenienced by the crowds, only enough were let in to comfortably occupy the seats.

The return trip was far more delightful to most of the tourists, than the one going.

That portion of California immediately north of San Francisco, we passed through in the night on our return trip, and when we awoke the morning after our start, we were in the midst of the beautiful Sacramento Valley. All day long we followed the curves of the Sacramento river and watched the restful, delightful views of nature's beauty, which constantly changed as the train curved in and out through the mountains. Two big wood-burning locomotives pulled us along with much puffing and groaning, and frequent stops to renew the wood from piles along the track. We passed the huts which the gold miners of '49 had abandoned, and looked with some curiosity at the remains of the placer apparatus, which they had used. There was little sign of life in those regions, which had made so many rich. The Sacramento river is a limpid stream, which looks as though it might be a furious torrent at times, but no one would suspect its hidden wealth.

Such trestles and curves as we passed over in climbing these mountains, we had never witnessed. Sometimes we would slowly crawl over a rickety looking wooden trestle, which seemed to span a ravine 150 feet deep. And the strange part of it was that the curve of the road most often occurred right where these bridges were. The long trains made them creak until we trembled lest we should be cast into the depths below.

Occasional glimpses we had of that most beautiful of American mountains, Shasta, but we did not arrive at the nearest point to its base until about noon. At Sisson we stopped for lunch, and there stood that symmetrical peak, clad in pure white, just in the background. We had seen loftier peaks, but none from such a low altitude. Over 14,000 feet she arose, and we were not over 3,000. Twenty-five miles away she stood, but the distance seemed but a stone's throw. Two peaks are visible, lifting their heads up proudly with not a wrinkle on their brows. A splendid specimen of mountain beauty. Seven extinct volcanoes could be seen from this point.

The ride through Oregon was enjoyed by everyone. The farming land was as fine as any seen on the trip, the farms were well kept, and there was an appearance of thrift on every hand. At Albany the farmers showed an enterprising spirit by bringing their fruits and other produce to the railroad station, where they placed it for the inspection of the Eastern travellers. It was a splendid show of agricultural products. In fact the whole party were quite enamored with Oregon, because of its apparent thrift, fertility, beauty of scenery and mild, equable climate.

Portland, with the splendid sail on the Columbia river; Tacoma and Seattle were all thoroughly enjoyed by the tourists. Unfortunately the time was cut so short at Portland that those who took the ride on the river, saw little of the city. The Christian Endeavorers of the city gave us a splendid welcome, and presented souvenirs to each of the tourists. But so anxious were most of the party to see the majestic Columbia, that they showed small appreciation of this thoughtfulness.

Portland is probably the most attractive city of the West. At least it appeals more forcibly to the Eastern traveller. It has magnificent residences, built more in the style of the East, and its location, especially the "Heights," is most charming. After reaching the summit on the cable cars, the view is magnificent. For miles the Williamette and Columbia can be seen, and four snow capped peaks are outlined against the sky in different directions. Hood, Rainier, Adams and St. Helens are all in full view, and there is no prettier quartet of peaks in the world.

The sail down the Williamette and up the Columbia was one which leaves such a restful, lasting impression. The Columbia seems more like the St. Lawrence than any other eastern river. It is four miles wide where Williamette enters it, and for many miles it flows between low banks fringed with small trees. But as we ascend it narrows, and the scenery along the banks is entrancing. We naturally compared it with our own lordly Hudson, and we were loath to give over the honors of the latter until we reached that magnificent part which corresponds to the palisades of the Hudson, and then we yielded. So picturesque were those cliffs rising up several hundred feet above the river, and surmounted by pinnacles and minarets, which add to their beauty. Castle Rock and Cape Horn were not only huge walls of rock, but were beautifully formed by the Divine architect. We came to the conclusion that this surpassed the Hudson, as the Hudson surpasses the Rhine. Time required that we should turn back ere we reached the still more picturesque cascades, and it was with sighs of regret that the bow of the steamer was turned down stream. All the way up the river we had grand old Mt. Hood right directly in front of us, sixty miles away when we first saw her, but seeming not more than five. Nothing could be more symmetrical than her perfectly white sides sloping down to river level from a height of 12,000 feet. But when the full moon rose over her snowy brow later in the evening, it was the most glorious vision one could imagine. It was nearly mid-night when we reached Portland, but the ride down the river by moon-light had been ideal, and a most delightful relief from dust and noise of the train.

The following morning we took breakfast at Tacoma, and spent a short time riding about the streets. Aside from Portland, we saw more of the art of the architect here than in any of the cities west of Minneapolis. There were beautiful residences scattered about on the hillside, which sloped down to Puget Sound. Many eastern people have homes in the town, we were told. It is a busy little place with large shipping interests.

While the train proceeded to Seattle, a two hours' ride, a small party of us made the distance by boat through the sound. It was a most delightful ride, and we learned to our surprise, from the captain, that the sound is never closed by ice in winter, and that there is very little snow on the ground in winter in Washington. The climate is moderated by the warm ocean currents.

Seattle is a typical western town. It lies on a hillside, and from the sound many streets could be seen, all overgrown with grass. The business part contains some very fine buildings. The Court House and school houses surpass those of equal towns in the east. But the residence portion is spread over a large acreage, with streets poorly kept, fences not in repair, no sidewalks, and with houses so irregular in size and style as to make one think that each one was built without any regard to the other. It has a most magnificent body of water in Lake Washington, which borders one side of the city. The parks on the lake side are very pretty. Seattle is a very busy place, many of the steamship lines from the Orient having their terminals here.

The scenery all through Washington and Idaho could not be surpassed for its beauties, and the Northern Pacific Railroad gave a service so far surpassing other roads which we passed over in the far West, that it was appreciated. With big locomotives we rushed through the mountains with a feeling of safety. Ravines, mountain peaks, magnificent groves, limpid streams, were the treat of this part of the journey.

We ate a most palatable breakfast at Spokane, on Saturday morning. The chief point of interest in this town are the falls in the Spokane river. The water converges from five different channels and leaps gracefully over the rocks to the bed below, a very pretty water scene.

At Missoula, in the heart of the Rocky Mountains, we

were welcomed with true western hospitality. The brass band was playing as we drew into the station, and carriages and omnibuses and horse cars drawn by mules were awaiting to convey us about the town. Everything was free to Christian Endeavorers in this mountain town. All work was laid aside and business was suspended in anticipation of the event. Even the bakers forgot to brew, as we could get no cake Saturday night that had been baked later than Tuesday. At the station a meeting was held, and several addresses made by Jerseymen and mountaineers.

Sunday was spent at Helena, with little satisfaction to any one, except that there were good services at the churches. It is a rough and tumble town, said to be the wealthiest in the country. We rode on streets that were literally paved with gold (the refuse of the gold mines) but we were glad when the time came to leave.

The next objective point was Livingston, Cinnabar and Mammoth Hot Springs in Yellowstone Park. What a grand day we had. Leaving Livingston at early morning, we reached Cinnabar before noon, and there took carriages for the Springs. It was a sight never before seen, so they told us, a string of 30 carriages, most with four horse teams and some with six. It was a glorious ride along that quiet, pensive, but beautiful Yellowstone. The mountains rose high on either side, and often the roadway was on the rocks jutting out from the side of the mountains with scarcely room for another vehicle to pass.

We dismounted at the Mammoth Hot Springs Hotel, and spent an interesting afternoon in roaming about among the hot springs, which have bubbled over the cliffs so long that the latter are converted into huge banks of crystal that have the appearance in the sunlight of big banks of snow piled on each other, and then dyed with streaks of rich brown and yellow and red. These formations from the springs are most wonderful. And the springs themselves as they bubble forth so hot from the rocks below that some of the party boiled eggs for their lunch in one of them, are a curious study. They make one feel strangely near the infernal regions. The strong smell of sulphur adds to this feeling. These springs are bubbling out everywhere, and the formations from the deposits of the water are extremely beautiful. We left the springs with regret in the early evening, and after a delightful ride back to our train, we were soon homeward bound, and the following morning had left the Rocky Mountains and all their grandeur far behind us.

Through the bad lands of Dakota, with all their curious formations, through the magnificent wheat fields of the same state into Minnesota, with her wealth of fertility and waterways. It was a ride not of grand mountain scenery, but of interest to everyone. Nothing can surpass that stretch of 2,000 miles spanned by the Northern Pacific, between Portland and St. Paul. We stopped at Minneapolis long enough to get a view of Minnehaha Falls, and a few of its splendid buildings, and then devoted the remainder of the time to St. Paul. Both of these cities had a tinge of eastern development entirely foreign to all the cities of the West.

Over the Northwestern route from St. Paul to Chicago is a beautiful ride which we did almost entirely in the night and reached Chicago early the following morning. Only a short stay there, and we were off on the homeward stretch, passing through some of the more fertile portions of Ohio and Indiana, which differed so much from the section crossed in going west that they seemed like other states. Not until we reached Cumberland, Va., did we retrace our westward tracks. But the ride over the Appallachian chain by daylight on the Baltimore and Ohio, was enjoyed by everyone, for the scenery is charming.

We arrived at Philadelphia early in the evening and there the South Jersey people left the train amid many adieus. At Trenton Junction another party left the train and a large number alighted at Bound Brook. All were glad to reach home, yet felt regrets at parting from their companions on such a wonderful journey.

The Scenery.

To describe the scenery of the trip is a most difficult task. The appreciation of the beauty, grandeur, or sublimity of nature is a matter of temperament. Knowing that what impressed me may have been unnoticed by others, I will make no attempt beyond a very general description, leaving the details to be filled in by each individual. Even a pen of a ready writer could not tell the story adequately, and besides, it would take more space than a book of this kind could accommodate. We are more or less familiar with the scenery east of the Alleghanies and hence attention is first directed to the rich farm lands of Ohio, Indiana, Illinois, Missouri and Kansas. We know now why the price of corn is low, and what it is that makes the western farmer rejoice when wheat takes a rise. There were acres of sage brush (which, by the way, has no botanical connection with grandmother's sage tea, or the sage flavored gravy which the Northern Pacific dining car served,) in Colorado and Utah and Nevada, less of it would have been just as interesting, but the oases that were formed by water from irrigating ditches, made it plain to us that these dry heaps of sand can be transformed into fertile gardens. Everywhere there were evidences that underneath the hills were millions of dollars worth of precious metals.

California was wonderland indeed. A place of perpetual

winter and a place of perpetual summer. We saw it and it was a garden; again we saw it and it was a desert. It was like a wheat field, an orchard, a vineyard, a pasture field. It is a land of natural contradictions, and the resources of this wonderful state will ever be praised by those to whom she gave such a hearty welcome. While we praise California, we must not forget Oregon and Washington. Such forests, farms, mountains, rivers, cities! Idaho, too, must have a share when praise is being distributed, for did she not squeeze her slender form between Washington and Montana, so that we might say we had been within her boundaries? The ranches of Montana confirmed in us a purpose of buying Montana horses, but Missoula's welcome seemed more real that Helena's wealth. Dakota took the eye of the tillers of the soil. Acres upon acres of rich, flat, farm land, and never a stone to interrupt the passage of the plow. Minnesota and Wisconsin showed us blackened stumps in great multitudes. They were monuments to the memory of millions of forest monarchs, who have given their lives to the lumber dealers in distant cities. This catalogue would not be complete with Minneapolis and St. Paul unmentioned. A resident of the latter place informed me, as his bosom swelled with manly pride, that "there are no horse cars in St. Paul, only electric cars." I heard no such advantages in Minneapolis. We saw Chicago too,—what magnificent scenery there is in the Northwestern and Baltimore and Ohio depot yards.

I must not forget, however, to tell the story of the great mountain ranges whose splendor had splendor added to them in the lofty peaks that arose here and there. Canons and gorges there were walled up with stupendous chunks cut or rolled from the mountain side. Forest trees towered heavenward, and at their feet thick underbrush growing among the rocks, made coverts for savage beasts, and hiding places for spotted snakes. The cliffs were set with starry speckles that told of gold and silver hidden beneath the rocky foundations. Rivers there were whose cascades sang merry songs, while boiling rapids raged and growled. The placid lakes showed their love for Dame Nature, by bearing her image in their bosoms, or helped the brightness of the sun by flashing his likeness from every ripple. Whether we beheld the dignified Mississippi, the big muddy Missouri, the reckless Arkansas which smoothed the wrinkles from every boulder that dared interrupt its passage; the mighty Sacramento, whose bed and banks of golden sand were appropriate guides for the course to the Golden Gate, or the Columbia, alive with luscious salmon, and laving with her silvery waters the peculiar pinnacles of rock that looked so weird as we took that moonlight ride; our tongues would cleave to the roof of our mouths because we could not speak. Let them cleave there if we ever forget these wonders!

The mountains are the most wonderful of all. Language cannot describe them. Human words are insufficient; they appeal to the inmost soul. Pike's Peak and Shasta and Hood and Jefferson and a dozen others are worthy of their places in fame. Their lofty peaks were white as snow untrodden by foot of man could be, save where some precipice, decorated with glistering crystals, showed its head through ice field and glacier. Silently and majestically their summits stood and pointed upwards like a huge finger guiding the eye to heaven, the dwelling place of Him who made the mountains. A cathedral wrapped in gloom may fill us with the sense of the presence of God, but we must adore His majesty and might, while under the spell of Shasta and her sisters.

The clear air was favorable to scenery. We never saw the stars so bright, nor the moon so silvery. As our train sped along the rails, and the evening shades began to fall, we could almost see the silence of the darkened crooks and crannies of the ravines. The trees were transformed into giants, the shrubbery into hobgoblins, and the flowers into elves and fairies. Nature outdid herself in the sunset in Dakota. The clouds were heavy, for the storm which broke upon us two hours later, in all the bluster of a western shower, was gathering. Just before the sun sank below the horizon, a rift in the clouds let the light through and filled the whole sky with radiancy. The rich green of the prairie was tinted with the brilliant scarlet and orange from on high. Lines of purple gold stretched from horizon to zenith. Here and there were masses of billowy cloud; their purple centres edged with golden feathers, and upholding pearly battlements decorated with gold and silver, fitting pinnacles indeed for the dome of heaven.

Having seen all this, and more, shall we not in the future love our native land better than before? Her natural beauty is the grandest in the world; her resources the richest beneath the skies. As never before we will sing:

> "I love thy rocks and rills,
> Thy woods and templed hills,
> My heart with rapture thrills,
> Like that above."

Living by the Way.

To tell of what, when and where we did our eating, ought not to prove an uninteresting chapter. Speaking generally we ate anything we could get, and were glad if we could get anything. We ate at all hours of the day and night. In respect to us, C. E. might be interpreted as Continually Eating. We ate wherever the train stopped, and it stopped everywhere. We were not particular how we ate; the thing to do was to eat, and to do it lively, or else get left. One spoon did for five or six, and the seventh stirred his coffee with his fork, that is provided he had a fork. One knife for each person was the rule, and as many butter knives as there were people. Manners were gone. No one pretended to do the thing in form. If he did, he did nothing else. Occasionally the crowd was rapped for a blessing, and the one blessing served to give thanks for what we were about to get, and what we had already eaten. One reverend gentleman was called upon to say grace when he was in the middle, the most interesting part, of his dinner. It was a question with him whether he should look forward, or back. Whether to be thankful for what he had already received, or what he still had in expectation. Being safe on the first proposition, he wisely confined himself to the second. Some ate their meals, if meals they could be called, on the folding bed. All beds fold in the West. Some dined off the stove, which was as cold as the coffee, and that was cold always. Others carried what they could grab into the Pullman and ate there, and then spent their time in looking for more. Eating was one of the stern problems of the excursion. All along the line, from Baltimore to the Golden Gate, the manna melted, no matter whether the sun struck it or not. One of the prophets says: "The wild ass, used to the wilderness, snuffeth up the wind at her pleasure." I can understand that now; there were some places where there was nothing else to "snuff up." Some days we dined on wind. Were glad to get it. Like the wild ass we became used to it. We have come to miss it. We didn't get fat on it, but we snuffed it.

Don't for a minute think I am trying to be funny. There wasn't anything funny in it. Breakfast at four o'clock in the afternoon only seems funny in print. In actual experience it ceases to be a joke. When there was any possibility of getting to a town, at some remote hour, we wired for something to eat, and, ordinarily, the whole population turned out to see us do it. The way we polished dishes seemed to amuse them. It was serious business for us. One section of the New York train followed in our wake for a number of miles. They always found the dining rooms swept and garnished. Swept clean of food and garnished with bones. I assume this became monotonous, for once they sent a telegram ahead beseeching that the Jersey crowd be not fed. Jersey fed all the same, and when the New Yorkers arrived, the Jerseymen were vanishing away, and with them every morsel of food to be had. New York has no further use for New Jersey. These are sober facts of history, undigested and disorderly it may be, but so is the food with which we are still encumbered. Once glad to be, but we are now converted. Various remedies, by patient application, may in time help matters. One minister preached on the convention after he returned, and among other things said, "I have just become used to one meal a day, and now I am under necessity of taking three." I understand from his wife that he was under no serious embarrassment. I suppose there ought to be some order in the narration of these things, but the dining was disorderly, and nothing falls into harmony.

C. E. stands for a lot of things we never thought of before. Cheese Eaters. Cookie Eaters. Cracker Eaters. Coffee Eaters, it was too thick to drink. Candy Eaters. Chicken Eaters. Cucumber Eaters. One Philadelphia minister will remember the cucumbers. Like the children of Israel, he lusted for them, and had a very narrow escape of being useful at Helena. In a more general sense, C. E. stands for other things. Clamorous Eaters. Circumspect Eaters, eating everything in sight and then looking around for more. Contented Eaters, the first in the dining room, notably certain ones from Belvidere, Salem, Washington, etc. The last might stand for Philadelphia and Newark. Curious Eaters, curious to know what they were eating. Deviled crabs at Baltimore puzzled the whole crowd; every one agreed that it was fish, and good, but none knew what sort of fish; possibly the mode of preparation accounts for their innocence. Then there were the Colored Eaters, no small contingent. These were the porters. They ate as if they were used to it. Speaking of the porters; one was left behind at a station; another porter remarked the he would soon catch up, as he saw him eating tomatoes. "What's that got to do with it?" somebody asks, and the porter replies, "Have you never heard of Tomato Ketchup?" At the time we regarded this as a thin joke. We were in no condition to appreciate it. Some of us will not soon forget one of these hungry looking porters at one of the eating stations in Utah. Breakfast was early that morning, that is if you are not mindful of being specially accurate, it was about 11:30 A. M. For some days this porter had evidently eaten nothing. He was obliged to keep fast days according to ancient traditions. The crowd was religious enough in this respect. This porter had an opportunity. The future was very uncertain. Like the camel of the desert, he made up his mind to take on a load for emergencies. He had before him a meat platter filled with baked beans, a favorite dish with the porters. They stay by you. In the middle of the platter was a huge piece of corned beef, say two pounds, fringed by at least four quarts of beans. The splendid way in which those beans dissolved before that darkie, would make a Chinaman and his chop-sticks blush. While the plate was being polished, the white eye-balls of the darkie were rolling around in search of something else; lovingly they came to rest on a suspicious looking pie; between beans, he called out nervously to the waiter, lest some one capture the pie before him, "Is dat pear pie, boss?" "Dunt no, I'll see" was the reply, and forthwith a long dirty finger was thrust under the crust, and out came a cherry. It was not pear pie, and under the circumstances not a very desirable cherry pie.

Speaking of Utah, no person on either of the Jersey sections will ever forget a place called Helper. The place is called Helper, because it is located at the beginning of a heavy grade, and ordinarily an additional engine is attached to the train to "helper" up the grade. We arrived there on Sunday morning. We had no intention of travelling on Sunday, but conscience weakened under the pangs of hunger. It was a work of necessity not to speak of mercy. We should have been in Salt Lake City on Saturday morning, but we were late, and that's no joke, for it was now

Sunday morning, and the Mormon city was still some twelve or fourteen hours ahead of us. Helper was not to be despised that Sunday morning. Four little houses and a small eating station, but this was superabundance to what we had grown accustomed. In about a minute after the train stopped, standing room in the eating room was at a premium, and the four little homesteads were literally swarming with hungry Jerseymen, and this includes women. It was the writer's fortune, with several clergymen, to get into one of these 8 by 12 rooms, which was flanked by a similar sized kitchen. One poor woman, a native, was doing her best in a bewildered way to supply the ham and eggs, which was the sole dish on the menu; they came slow, so slow that one of the ministers, about six feet tall, you all know him, out of tender sympathy for the poor body at work, or more likely from a suspicion that he would get left, decided to "helper," and himself as well. So it happened that at about the time he might have been ascending the pulpit in his own church, he was standing before that red hot kitchen stove, frying ham and eggs. He had no monopoly, for soon two other clergymen had gone into the same business, and ere long they were the picture of contentment, as they leisurely stored away the provender so secured. I have, perhaps, said a little too much about ministers in this article, but it is because they were much in evidence. It is possibly characteristic when it becomes a question of eating. There was one man on our section, I don't know his name, but he was known to some of us under the name of Coffee. We called him that because he took coffee wherever we stopped. In a mild way I should say that he drank enough coffee to supply a ship canal between New York bay and San Francisco harbor. Milk was the most generally consumed article of diet.

The quantity of it that was gathered into those Pullmans in all sorts of vessels would certainly float the United States navy. I never saw the like of it. Some people had nothing else. Whenever the train had passed a station, all the cows in the neighborhood thought it was a cyclone. I understand they have declined to give any more milk for a month.

Some people started with huge baskets filled with eatables. A precaution that was fully justified in experience. One of my friends, by no means an inexperienced traveller, my companion on this trip, turned up his nose at these baskets. He said, "I can't abide these cold meals; the smell of hard boiled eggs and dry ham sandwiches always make me sick." I agreed with him, and we started with nothing in reserve. By the time we arrived in Salt Lake City, we were both properly converted, and on Monday morning you could have seen two chastened Endeavorers going softly through the streets of the Mormon city, and quietly loading two great baskets. I fail to remember all that was in them; a chafing dish, plates, cups, saucers, knives, forks, spoons, salt, pepper, bread, butter, fresh eggs, canned meats, chipped beef, cheese, coffee, sugar, condensed milk, etc. We entered our car with the satisfied reflection that we would starve no more. Like some other things, this is much more fine in print than in experience. The first meal was a great success. It was breakfast. We prepared it together. Soft boiled eggs. Frizzled beef in condensed milk (a little sweet). Bread and butter, coffee. What more do you want? As I said we prepared that meal together, and were both satisfied, but lost our enthusiasm in doing the cooking; we made the porter wash the dishes. We decided to take turns at cook. When he cooked the meals were excellent, to him; when I cooked they were all right, for me. If the thing had gone on we couldn't have continued good friends, so we gave up the whole outfit, reserving the chafing dish to the porter. On the basis of our munificent donation the porter set up the business and charged us ten cents a cup for coffee; business increased with astonishing rapidity, and soon the porter of the car ahead was in partnership with ours; out of the profits the capital stock was increased sufficiently to warrant the purchase of two oil stoves and additional cups and spoons; if the trip had gone on much further the George & Benjamin Franklin Co. would have had a chattel mortgage on all of us. It was a costly experiment, but wisdom is always expensive, and especially so when, like Jacob, you get it by experience. I could write much more, but I am limited in space, and have already far exceeded that which was allotted to me. I can only say in conclusion, if hereafter any hot blooded, youthful Endeavorers want to travel through the wild and wooly West on a New Jersey section, with nothing to eat but a vision of prairie dogs, they are welcome to it, but as for me, my delight is with the sons of men who know enough to travel on trains that carry a dining car.

Sleeping Car Contemplations.

There were personal reasons for my thinking much about our sleeping accommodations. We were nine successive nights in our car going, and as many returning. Usually my bed was the last one made; although I was the longest sleeper on the car.

One morning I borrowed a measuring rule of an engineer and took the length and breadth of my boudoir. As I am six feet and three inches from scalp to the tendon of Achilles, I thought of the Scripture, "the bed was shorter than a man could stretch himself upon it." It proved to be six feet two inches "short," and two feet ten inches "narrow," with less than three feet space between berths when ready for the night. I occupied alone the lower berth of the eighteenth section.

A double-hinged door presumably separated my section and the opposite one from the rest of the car, but was kept open twenty-three hours and thirty minutes of the twenty-four. These two sections became the main sitting room and reception room of our caravansary on wheels. A continuous aisle ran from platform to platform.

The gentlemen, last to retire, lingered around our made or unmade bed until 11 o'clock, and often later, for reasons best known to themselves. This shortened my hours of sleep at the beginning. Then there was a well-meaning rustic who was afflicted with the disease of early rising, and who, for my interest in sleep, the gods be praised, left us for an extended tour of Yellowstone Park. He was usually at the laver before 4:30 A. M. splashing like a duck, puffing like a porpoise, and talking like a windmill.

At 11 P. M. the gas was turned nearly off, and you could glance down a dim corridor, two feet wide, formed btween continuous curtains for sixty feet, and about eight feet high.

Each lower berth gave the occupant or occupants an undisputed right to nearly sixty cubic feet of air. Each upper berth had more, because of the unobstructed space between the pillow and the dome of the car. The tribulations of an excursionist can not be fully described. A vivid imagination will complete what can neither be written nor kodacked. When some who had the courage, born of their surroundings, attempted to lay aside some of their travel-stained garments before getting between the sheets, the scene was variegated. Persons behind opposite curtains on a two feet aisle, trying to partially disrobe upon a lurching car, with porter and passengers passing momentarily, will find themselves in peculiar, and sometimes painful contacts. The avoirdupois upon your feet, or the momentum with which your fifth rib comes in contact with the side of the berth, or your cranium collides with the ceiling, you have neither time nor temper to calculate with mathematical exactness. And sometimes nolens volens, a motion of the car, peoples the corridor with more than an occasional animated robe de nuit, pajama or jeagris most approved. The conditions which would, in well regulated homes, shock the sense of propriety and cause scamperings, are simply inevitable. But as all are sharers in the situation, with commendable equanimity, we rush to cover, if only with the success of an ostrich.

The effort of the uninitiated to get into a berth for the first time, will not be forgotten. If after two or three attempts to get into bed and get the proper extremity upon the pillow, and especially into an upper berth from the top of a narrow and uncertain step ladder, you succeed, you are to be congratulated. More than one man had an upper berth in a section in which the lower was occupied by ladies, whose acquaintance he had made upon the car. For a timid man, the situation presented new problems. How shall he make the simplest preparation for the night, such as unlacing his shoes? Shall he sit upon the floor in the aisle and be trodden upon; or upon the edge of the lower berth wherein are the ladies, or unwilling even to part the curtains, try to climb over the pole and roll into his berth, shoes and all? And into their berths these bashful men generally went as presentable as when they appeared in our car parlor before breakfast.

So far I have spoken of facts visible, but behind the curtains are invisible fact and fancy. It is impossible to reconcile our ideas of godliness and cleanliness with keeping on the same garments night and day for several successive days, even on a journey. Shoes must be unlaced and garments removed. And a person must be considerably undersize who can sit upright in a lower berth. A man must hump his back and spring up until his curved spine strikes the upper berth in order to get his coat skirts from under him. And it will require several efforts of this kind for securing results, which are complicated by the situation. Then he must practice the long neglected feat of his boyhood, called "skinning the cat," to get all the way out of coat and other garments. But particulars can not be given in detail. But extended arms secure bruised knuckles, and strained positions are uncomfortable. Sometimes the whole body must be lifted from the mattress, until only the head and feet touch. Various necessities in disrobing require the repetition of this beautiful feat in athletics. Within our limited space these motions of the body requiring the skill of a gymnast, have been required by male and female, old and young. It was often felt, if not expressed, "this pent up Utica does so contract our powers." Possibly the trials of the ladies, for the same causes, were more than those of the gentlemen. One of their serious complaints was the brass ornament at the lock of the upper berth. It was asserted that a thrifty porter could set up a hair establishment and provide a switch with the color of the hair of every lady on his car.

And morning comes after the longest night. To become invested with that of which we have been divested, is in many respects attended with greater difficulties. The matter of arranging the toilet was more complicated where two occupied a berth. The ladies who did this had our sympathies, and we commend them for their neat appearance and true womanliness under all circumstances. A brother minister had an upper berth. The lower was occupied by two ladies first met on the car. It seemed imperative to prepare for the night as well as for the day upon the narrow area and cramped positions of his sleeping place. He had to disappear in full dress and reappear in the morning as presentable as possible. Not enjoying the situation he wanted to share my berth. And I was compelled to refuse his request. But why? Because he was fat and I was long. The shortness of my bed compelled me to lie bias, or as a Xtian scientist would say, diagonally. Either W. would have had to curl himself in the corner at my head or feet, or our bodies would have formed an X, with the point of contact amid-ships. In this last adjustment each could only get his half of the bed by lying on both sides of the other fellow.

But humor aside the Pullman was a great comfort. Even a contracted sleeping place was indispensable. Here we found tired nature's sweet restorer. As we think of some things here intimated, and of some we have not ventured to describe, which were even more amusing, we will have happy thoughts of the companions of our great excursion, or laugh and perhaps grow fat.

The Devotional Meetings on the Train.

It is said that Sir William Cecil, when he was lord-treasurer of England, would sometimes throw off his official gown, and say, "lie there, lord-treasurer." The truly pious cannot throw off their religion and say, "Lie there, Christian." Their religion is not a garment. It is a life. It is not put on and off. It is put in and out. It is just as natural for the Christian to give light and sweetness and joy, as it is for the star to shine, the rose to breathe, and the bird to sing. The New Jersey Christian Endeavorers did not wear their religion, as a robe, to San Francisco, but they used it as a life. Chapters of evidence might be submitted. A few fragments must suffice.

Just after we left the state of New Jersey, a young lady on the second section of our train became ill. Her travelling companion was a young lady whom she had never met before; but in her she found a faithful friend, a patient, cheerful and wise nurse, who sacrificed with joy and served with devotion. The most beautiful friendship is when Jesus Christ welds the links of heaven's gold. The most perfect service is where He lives in a human soul. At the railroad stations this Christian Endeavor nurse might be seen trying to purchase delicacies for the sick one. At many of the points of interest she remained on the car with her patient, and, through all this, there was not the sound of a murmur.

She made us think of Jesus. So did others, because there were similar instances of exemplary fidelity. It was not at all unusual to see Christian Endeavorers reading their Bibles every day. A bright, consecrated Endeavorer found delight in arranging a Bible class for Sunday. When she could not get one teacher, because he had been at Pike's Peak, and ——————, with charming perseverance, she worked until she secured another.

Each day, about 7:30 p. m., the passengers and delegates, being invited, would assemble in different cars, where helpful services were held. The leaders were usually selected from the numerous clergymen on board. The meetings were opened with inspiring songs. The leader would then make a prayer, which was followed by singing, and this in turn by reading a portion of Scripture. Then came a brief address, more singing, and then the Christian Endeavorers would recite passages of Scripture and speak. Certainly it was difficult at times to conduct these meetings. There is a vast difference between a fast, flying train and a comfortable church edifice, but some could hear, all could participate, and God could understand. Sometimes opportunities were afforded for holding services at the stations, where the train was to remain for awhile. These opportunities were eagerly embraced. Persons residing near the stations seemed delighted to hear the singing, prayers and remarks. The station-masters would cheerfully consent to the holding of the services, and, when it was possible, they and the railroad men generally attended. At one of these stations there was found a large Mormon population. The superintendent of the primary department of the Bethany Presbyterian Sunday School, who was en route to San Francisco with us, taught the little Mormon children an impressive Sunday School lesson.

At the close of the lesson she made a tender appeal to the children, and they held up their hands for prayer. The effect of this meeting was somewhat spoiled by a ludicrous blunder on the part of a zealous clergyman from New Jersey. He thought it would be an excellent idea to have the children sing at the close of the services. Accordingly he selected from a Mormon hymnal, a song beginning with a reference to Christ. Without reading the entire stanza, he promptly requested the children to sing that hymn. They agreed to do so. When the prayer was ended they began to sing with voices clear, sweet and ringing, and each stanza closed with, "I'll be a little Mormon and follow Brigham Young." There is a moral here transparently clear.

At another station among the eager spectators was an old lady, who said she had come a long distance to see the Christian Endeavorers. She told us in her plaintive way that she lived so far from even the nearest church, out in that prairie land, that it was impossible for her to attend divine services, and that she had not heard a sermon for many years. "Please sing to me," said she, and the Christian Endeavorers sang, as only they can sing when their hearts are so deeply moved, "How Firm a Foundation, ye Saints of the Lord." When the following stanza: "E'en down to old age all my people shall prove, my sovereign, eternal, unchangeable love," etc., was being sung, the train started, and the good old woman lifted her thin, pale hand, and with tears streaming down her time-furrowed cheeks, she said: "God bless you, my children! Do not forget that you helped the old woman on the prairies." It was worth a trip across the continent to be of service to such a soul; and receive the benediction of that saint. Although she has been deprived of the public worship of God, she has grown ripe and beautiful in the sunshine of His immediate presence. Shall we meet her again at life's last station, and will she then sing to us a song of the ransomed in that sweet, summer land above; and then shall we go up together to praise Him who makes His service so blessed?

It was carefully planned that we should reach Salt Lake City before Sunday; but this, under the circumstances, was impossible. Very much to the regret of all concerned, it became necessary to run the train until late Sunday afternoon. This was due, as all will understand, to the fact that so many trains were on the road, and that we were first blocked and then pushed. Under ordinary circumstances our consciences would have been crushed between the wheels and the tracks, and the rumbling wheels would have said, "Thou art condemned." But instead of this we made the wheels rumble praises to God, and we turned the cars into churches. Daily devotional services were also held in some of the hotels at San Francisco, and it was a familiar sound to hear the Endeavorers on street cars singing happy Christian songs. When the convention was ended and once again we all met on the train, it really seemed like a family reunion, and our altar of prayer was fragrant with thanksgiving. The loved ones at home were always remembered in prayer, both as we were going and as we were returning. On the "homeward bound" we spent Sunday at Helena, Mon. The New York delegates were also there, and the ministers of New York and New Jersey filled the pulpits of the Helena churches at the morning services. In the afternoon a mass-meeting was held, and Rev. Cortland Myers, D. D., delivered an earnest address. Another mass-meeting took place in the evening, and Rev. J. Wilbur Chapman, D. D., who was with the New Jersey delegates, delivered a sermon of great power. Services were continued at every possible place, and at the most opportune time, until the last day ended. We had just eaten dinner at the Queen City Hotel, Cumberland, Md., when Rev. Dr. Chapman stood on the long porch in front of the hotel, and, with the Endeavorers all around him, he conducted a most impressive farewell meeting. He announced at this time that services would be held with a sick lady on one of the cars. This meeting took place just after we left Cumberland, and it was followed by another farewell service, conducted by the Rev. T. E. Davis. Mr. Davis read an appropriate Psalm, and devoutly acknowledged the gracious protection of Almighty God, and His divine aid granted unto the chairman of the Transportation Committee in all his arduous duties.

In addition to the benefits already mentioned as derived from these meetings, there were many others. There were persons on the excursion who were not Christian Endeavorers, and some of them were not even Christians. It was perfectly evident the Christians were edified, and that others were deeply impressed. The brakemen sometimes attended, and the porters, also, were usually present. There are reasons for believing that these men received permanent profit. Some of them are members of the churches where they reside, but their vocations preclude the possibility of their being present very often at the divine services. They were like thirsty souls drinking at fountains pure and cool. Some of the popular Christian Endeavor songs became favorites with the unconverted, and they frequently requested us to sing them. The writer is acquainted with a man who seldom, if ever, attended church when he was home. One day we were singing, "What a Friend We Have in Jesus," and some one stepped to the side of the writer, took hold of his book, and began to sing very heartily. He turned and looked, and it was that man. A subsequent conversation proved that the good seed had not fallen in unprolific soil. Moreover, the reflex influence upon the Endeavorers themselves was most wholesome. They were abundantly benefited. Life, love and duty triumphed. The greatest thing in the world is life. The greatest thing in life is love. The greatest thing in love is duty. Life is the seed, love is the stem, and duty is the blooming flower.

The Christian Endeavorers on the New Jersey Special did their duty. But, above all, God was glorified. Religion was exemplified as something beautiful, joyous, attractive. The seeds of Christ's harvest were scattered. We cannot account for all. Some are hidden. They shall germinate, grow and ripen. In the harvest day, by and by, shall we find sheaves that we did not know of, that we did not expect? Probably.

The Convention.

To the writer of this article has been assigned the duty of writing up "The Convention of Young Peoples' Society of Christian Endeavor," which was held in San Francisco, July 7 to 12, 1897. But where shall the writer begin; where end? What shall he include; what leave out? To give even a synopsis of all the addresses delivered at the various meetings, would be to make a good sized volume; to select this or that address and particularize, will be to invite criticism as to judgment, and yet in pursuance of duty we may be led to brave that.

How can he convey in language the enthusiasm that was apparent, or paint in words the deep spiritual undercurrent that was felt, although unseen? Two elements that were present, and which combined to stamp the convention as one of the best, if not the best, ever held; for from the opening session on Thursday morning, July 7, to the close of the one on Monday evening, July 12, the convention moved forward with ever increasing enthusiasm and spiritual power; true there was one or more breaks in the program, caused by sickness, but the breaks were so skilfully bridged by those in charge, that there was no apparent check to the enthusiasm, or loss to the spiritual power with which the convention was carried forward.

The various addresses of welcome tended to start the convention on a high plane, and from the many we make selections. The one delivered by Mr. R. V. Watt, Chairman of the Convention Committee contains these words:

"We welcome you therefore because you are seeking to present the Savior of man to the world that the world may be made better.

"We welcome you for your own sakes; your buoyant enthusiasm, your thoughtful earnestness, your calm determination, your intelligence, your integrity, your sincerity, your consecration to a great cause, commands our admiration, begets our love, and makes us your willing servants.

"We welcome you because of the millions of young people devoted to good citizenship, temperance and righteousness whom you represent.

"We welcome you because we believe you will be among our people 'living epistles known and read of all men,' and that thereby the youth of our sundown country may be inspired to greater zeal in all right effort.

"We welcome you because we believe your coming will direct the thoughts and attention of our young people to higher and holier things, and because many lives will be made better and more useful by what shall be uttered by those who will occupy the platform from day to day,"

From the one delivered by Rev. J. K. McLean, D. D., who spoke for the pastors of the Golden Gate, we quote as follows:

"My friends, it gives us new courage when we realize by the presence of such a gathering as this the mighty forces of prayer and sympathy and work and love that we have behind us, and it gives us greater assurance in those visions of the future when we comprehend—as we cannot, except by ocular demonstration—the incarnation of Christianity in our own and other lands; it gives us hopes of the recruits we are to receive by and by, those who are to be co-workers with us and our successors in this work. Therefore it gives us great gladness to see you here to-day. We ask of you to look upon our foundations; we ask of you to leave your sympathy, your prayers, your love and your undying interest here."

The annual address of President Clark, which was delivered in the opening session, was characteristic of the man. Broad in conception and catholic in spirit, encircling the world with the Gospel of Christ.

His theme was as follows:

"A world-encircling religious movement; how shall it fulfill God's design?"

In the address, when alluding to the movements of the Lord's hosts going forth conquering, and still to conquer, we have these words:

"This is a world movement, thank God, away from materialism, formalism and a barren ecclesiasticism, back to God himself. It is the 'Spirit of life,' the 'life hid with Christ in God,' the life emptied of self and surrendered to God. Of this movement Christian Endeavor is a part, vitalized by it, and on its part, contributing to it;" and then follows this injunction:

"Endeavorers, let this be the motto, the purpose, the prayer of this coming seventeenth year; to come within the blessed reach of this current, to abide in Christ, to surrender ourselves to Him, to let Him use us, to think less of our efforts and more of His fullness; to seek a larger infilling from above, deeping draughts of His life, more emptiness of self, more fulness of Christ."

Equally interesting and impressive was the annual report of the General Secretary, J. Willis Baer, from which, for future reference, we quote. There are at present 50,780 local societies of Christian Endeavors, with a membership of 3,000,000.

Referring to the movement throughout the world he said:

"England has 3,925 societies; Australia, 2,124; Scotland, 433; Wales, 311; India, 250; Ireland, 169; Madagascar, 93; France, 68; Mexico, 100; Japan, 66; West Indies, 63; Turkey, 41; China, 53; Africa, 52; Germany, 32, and so on through a long list, with a total of 7,919 societies. In addition, all Canada has 3,390 societies."

Alluding to the interdenominational spirit of the movement, he gave the following:

"In the United States the Presbyterians are more numerous than any other, there being 5,531 Young People's societies and 2,934 Junior societies. The Congregationalists are next, with 4,156 Young People's and 2,407 Junior; the Disciples of Christ third, numbering 3,208 Young People's societies and 1,322 Junior; Baptists, 2,640 Young People's societies and 1,080 Junior; Cumberland Presbyterian, 867 Young People's societies and 361 Junior; Methodist Protestants, 971 Young People's societies and 251 Junior; Lutherans, 869 Young People's and 324 Junior, and so on, until we have enumerated nearly forty different varieties.

"In Canada, the Methodists lead with 1,062 Young People's societies and 170 Junior; Presbyterians, 1,056 Young People's societies and 146 Junior; Baptists, 168 Young People's societies and 35 Junior.

"In the United Kingdom the Congregationalists, with 1216, lead the Baptists by only 6 societies. Then the Presbyterians and Primitive Methodists follow. Under the Southern Cross, in Australasia, the Western Methodists are the most numerous."

Speaking of the increase in Missionary spirit he stated that:

"A 'missionary roll of honor' will be unrolled in one of our meetings next Monday. Upon it are the names of 10,468 Christian Endeavor societies that have given nearly $200,000 to missions through their own denominational mission boards. And these same societies have given an equal amount for other benevolences. The largest gift to missions reported by any one society is $1,437.01, of the Clarendon street Baptist Society of Boston. The Calvary Presbyterian Society of Buffalo is second, with $1,016.85.

"And we must take off our hats to a Chinese society here in San Francisco, the one in the Chinese Congregational Mission. It stands third, having given nearly $700 to its own denominational missionary board, and is supporting six missionaries in the field."

But best of all, he said: "During the last year 25,264 of the Juniors have joined the church, and 187,125 from the Senior department; in all, 213,385." Truly a host ransomed, and for which the church of God may well thank Him and praise His holy name.

The evangelistic thought was emphasized this year, and many services were held in different parts of the city, under the leadership of such men as Rev. J. Wilbur Chapman, D. D., of Philadelphia; Rev. Ford. Ottman, of Newark, N. J.; Rev. R. Y. Pierce, of Philadelphia, who had at their command a host of workers.

In addition to the evangelistic services, which formed a part of the program of the convention, the Committee of Arrangements had introduced some special services which were instructive, helpful and inspiring. Such was the "Daily hour for Bible study," from 8:30 to 9:15 A. M., in the Central M. E. Church, conducted by one of the best of

Bible teachers, Prof. Herbert L. Willett, of Chicago. Here many found their way from day to day to learn the method of teaching, and obtain clearer knowledge of the word taught.

Another very helpful service was the "Quiet Hour" from 4:30 to 5:30 in the afternoon; this meeting was held in the Calvary Presbyterian Church, under the leadership of Mr. W. C. Studd, of London, Eng., assisted by Dr. Chapman, of Philadelphia. How restful the hours spent in this place; how helpful to the deepening of spiritual life were the talks given by these men of God. How strengthening and inspiring for service was the consciousness of the presence of the Holy Spirit.

The hour from 8:30 to 9:15 every morning in the First United Presbyterian Church, was an attractive one for many; for here was to be found Rev. R. F. Y. Pierce, of Philadelphia, with his bit of magic chalk, showing the practical use of the black board in Christian work. How quickly the hour slipped away as we watched his hand and listened to his talk. We give one of his illustrations which was heard by many: "Sin shatters so many precious and noble lives; God meant that our hearts should be full of glee; that our hearts should be laughing and full of song." In two seconds he drew a big heart in outline, and with a few strokes he put in eyes, nose and a laughing mouth. "Then," said he, "the devil came along and turned the laugh upside down and put lines of care in the face," and while he said it with a dash of his chalk, the mouth was reversed and the suggestion of a countenance was a picture of woe. He continued: "The Devil comes and shatters our joy. David once sang, 'in thy presence, O God, is fulness of joy,' but David's note of joy was changed." While he was speaking, there appeared a section of a staff of music, and above it a dark cloud of sin. Suddenly a lightening bolt shot from the cloud, shattering a bar, and the note of "Joy" dropped out. The lesson was impressive and not readily forgotten.

"Men see the truth," said Mr. Pierce, "they may forget the words, but they never forget the picture; to me it is so simple that I marvel that a few ministers are doing it."

Another new feature of this convention was the service on Sunday afternoon in the First United Presbyterian Church for boys and girls. This meeting was led by J. Willis Baer. In this meeting over 1,500 children, from the little tot of four years, to the boy of fifteen, were gathered, filling the entire audience room. Here came Dr. Pentecost to talk to them on "My son, give me thine heart." How pleasing his manner as he told them how, if they gave their hearts to God, they would place their bodies as well as their souls in the keeping of the Creator. Here also Mr. C. N. Hunt, the converted lawyer, who has given up his practice of law to do the work of an evangelist, was pressed into service. How intent was the attention of the audience as he told them of Jesus, and urged them to "Try and be like Jesus."

While this meeting was going on, there was also one like it in spirit being held in Woodward's pavilion for men only; conducted by Dr. Chapman, assisted by Rev. F. C. Ottman. The latter in his address laid great stress upon the value of faith. "Religious belief," he said, "could not always be based upon reason, because God's ways are inscrutable, and man's range of vision limited." Citing Israel crossing Jordan as illustrating his thought. His address, although short, was a fitting prelude to the one which followed by Dr. Chapman, who spoke on "Dissipation, Infidelity and Morality."

The Doctor's address was practical, tending to arouse conscience. At the close of his remarks he asked all of those who felt the need of living a better life, and wished him to pray for them, to raise their hands. All over the great audience hands were raised. And then followed the prayer so full of tenderness; so full of yearning for salvation for these, that many hearts were touched, as was manifest by the wet eyes when prayer was ended.

Simultaneous with this meeting for men, was one for women only in the First Congregational Church, to which the women came in such numbers as to fill the church to overflowing, many being content to remain in the outer hall, being unable to get any farther. The meeting was conducted by Mrs. F. E. Clark, who, under the providence of God was enabled to make it one that those present will not soon forget.

Among the speakers was Mrs. V. E. Mathews, of New York, who spoke in behalf of her race, the Afro-American women; how intently that vast audience listens as she speaks.

Thanking God for His boundless love, which included her and her race in the plan of salvation, she added: "All the more are we grateful to the moral and Christian forces of the world, the Christian statesmen and soldiers and scholars, who were the divine instruments, making it possible for this womanhood to stand in this august presence to-day."

What one of that great throng will ever forget the object lesson on Missions that Mrs. Clark gave them, when placing a little Chinese girl on the reading desk, she said: "Unless this little girl is rescued, she will be sold as a slave; her life will be one of hardship and degradation; her fate seems almost too dreadful to contemplate." What a thrill went through that vast audience. "Sold as a slave! and in this country!" they cried. Ah, yes, they of the Pacific Slope knew this too well; but those of the East, to them it was something they had read about, but could scarcely belief it to be so. But now their sad faces and streaming eyes told volumes. To them that little girl was a practical lesson in Home Missionary work; henceforth they would aid their sisters in the slope of the Pacific to rescue such as these, and would follow their gifts with their prayers.

The addresses during the convention were of the same high order as of former years. How could they be otherwise with the speakers that addressed the convention. They being Rev. Josiah Strong, D. D., Rev. B. B. Tyler, D. D., Rev. George F. Pentecost, D. D., Rev. Silas Mead, LL. D., Rev. Matt. S. Hughes, D. D., Rev. R. Y. Pierce, Rev. J. W. Chapman, D. D., Rev. F. E. Clark, D. D., and others. The consecration services on Monday evening, brought the convention to a close. At the one in Mechanics' Pavilion, Rev. F. E. Clark presided, and Rev. G. F. Pentecost, D. D., preached the sermon. Dr. Pentecost is a magnetic talker, and enforced his arguments with the strongest reasons.

The consecration service which followed, was conducted by Dr. Clark, and consisted in roll call of states. The answer of our state being: "He shall have dominion from sea to sea, and from the river unto the end of the earth," and one verse of "my faith looks up to Thee." The meeting held in Woodward's Pavilion, had as its presiding officer, J. Willis Baer, and Dr. J. W. Chapman as preacher. Here, as in Mechanics' Pavilion, the audience filled the building to overflowing.

The preacher urged upon his hearers a closer walk with God, and exhorted the Endeavorers to put forth every effort to come closer to Him, not only in the consecration service, but in their whole lives.

He made a strong and eloquent plea for a fearless upholding of the banner of Jesus Christ.

The service for consecration to the service of Christ began with silent prayer by the vast audience, after which Secretary Baer exhorted all present to let their light shine, and thereby let the world know that they had given their hearts, their souls, to God. The roll of states was then called and responses, same as in the other building, were given. Then followed the benediction, and the sixteenth annual convention of the Christian Endeavor was adjourned.

San Francisco.

San Francisco has been enshrined within the hearts of the nearly five hundred delegates from New Jersey, who attended the "Sixteenth National C. E. Convention," lately held in the city by the "Golden Gate."

San Francisco originally comprised two villages, Yerba Buena and Dolores. They were united under one name in 1847.

Fifty years ago only four hundred and fifty persons lived within the present bounds of the city.

The discovery of gold in 1848, caused an excitement similar to that of to-day, resulting from the discovery of gold in the Klondike regions. Multitudes flocked thither from every nation, clime and tongue! The city sprang up as if by magic. This marvelous growth has continued until San Francisco stands among the leading cities of the world, with a population of about 330,000.

Well has San Francisco been called the "City of the Hundred Hills." These hills are from two hundred to six hundred feet in height. The streets are laid out at right angles to each other, and run over the hills, instead of around them, as one might expect. Thus are these hills terraced on every side.

The city enjoys the best street car service in the world. As the cable car glides rapidly and smoothly down one of the steepest streets with the eyes closed, one can easily imagine himself enjoying a toboggan slide.

The "Broadway" of the metropolis of the Pacific slope, is Market street. It extends from the sea wall, directly through the heart of the city to the bay. Nearly all the principal street car lines converge in it.

Many are the interesting and costly buildings seen by visitors within the city's gates. Among the most imposing structures is the Palace Hotel, built at great cost, and covering two and a half acres of ground. Its inner court is of Spanish design, roofed with glass one hundred and fifty feet above. White enamelled columns support the galleries, which surround the court. At night the sight is most beautiful, when lighted up by a multitude of incandescent lamps.

The new City Hall stands near Mechanic's Pavilion, the headquarters of the Convention. It is still in course of construction. When completed it will cost $4,000,000. It covers six and three-quarters acres. Its dome points heavenward, farther than that of the Capitol at Washington.

The palatial residences of aristocratic San Francisco on Nob Hill, are among the most capacious, elegant and costly in the world.

Public buildings, including libraries, schools and churches have been erected throughout the city, without the sparing of expense.

At the foot of Nob Hill, on the east, is the Chinese portion of the city, "Chinatown." It is one of the greatest curiosities to visitors. Instead of its being a suburb of the city, as most strangers suppose, it occupies four or five blocks in the very heart of the city. By crossing a street, one steps from the fashionable world into a transplanted bit of China. Here 30,000 Chinamen are huddled together in quarters which would not accommodate one-fifth that number of Americans. They have brought with them all the habits and ways of life of the mother country.

They have their theatres, joss-houses, opium joints, gambling dens and places of business, all conducted in the Chinese fashion.

Were you in "Chinatown" on the Sabbath? If so, it did not seem at all like the Christian Sabbath. Though living in the very heart of one of the finest cities on the globe, these heathen people are allowed to do and to live about as they please. The Sabbath is desecrated by a continuous buying and selling. Some of their wares exposed for sale, especially their dried and smoked meats are almost nauseating to look upon.

Slavery was abolished by the United States a third of a century ago. But alas, in the heart of San Francisco there exists a slavery ten thousand times more degrading and terrible than that of which mention has been made.

A noted writer for the "Golden Rule," in speaking of this great curse, says: "One would have to go to perdition to find language in any sense adequate to describe the enormity of human slavery as seen in "Chinatown," where behind screens girls and young women are denied their liberty."

A few years ago the cry was: "San Francisco needs the Convention." She has had it. May our dear heavenly Father so bless the holding of the Convention in that city that this crying shame and dark blot of infamy may be wiped out, and forever!

Notwithstanding the abominable and heathenish practices of "Chinatown," all is not dark. In the Christian services held in the various Chinese chapels, and the seed sown in the Sabbath Schools, as witnessed by some of the

C. E. delegates, the "leaven" is seen to be surely working. A blessed work is being done at the Presbyterian "Rescue Mission for Girls."

Many are the places of interest in the outskirts of the city. Among these are the Sutro Baths. They are in an immense amphitheatre, covered with glass, affording accommodations for eight thousand persons. One may enjoy either hot or cold, salt or fresh water bathing. These baths are the finest in the world, and were built by one of San Francisco's benevolent citizens, a Jew and an ex-Mayor.

Sutro Gardens were laid out and built by the same person. They are filled with costly semi-tropical plants and flowers. Well kept drives and walks thread the grounds. Costly statuary is found in various parts of the garden, among the shrubbery and in secluded nooks, as well as in the more prominent portions. A most interesting museum attracts the attention of the visitor.

Sutro Heights afford an extensive view of the Pacific Ocean, perhaps the finest to be obtained by the traveler anywhere on the California coast.

The ride to the Cliff House from any part of the city, either by steam or electric cars, is truly charming. Some of the New Jersey party went out by street car lines and returned on the steam cars, keeping nearer the coast and passing round the rocky hinge of the Golden Gate. The Cliff House is a large hotel built upon the projecting rocks at Point Lobos. The waves dash in spray against the rocky foundation of this much frequented resort.

But a short distance out in the ocean are the celebrated Seal Rocks, consisting of a few immense boulders rising out of the waters.. Many sea lions are seen upon these rocks, basking in the sun.

One of the principal points of interest, which every visitor should see, is the Golden Gate Park. But a few years ago the site of this beautiful paradise was but a desert waste of sand. Hundreds of acres have been converted into a garden where flowers bloom the year around. There are picturesque bridges, waterfalls, ponds, fountains, and parks for animals. In the extensive conservatory are palms, ferns, orchids and other tropical plants. A magnificent observatory on Strawberry Hill gives a fine view of sea, mountain and city. Delightful were the few days spent in the Convention City by the Golden Gate. The Golden Gate, itself, is a fascinating point of interest. It is a mile in width, through which passes much of the commerce of the Eastern world. It was thus most appropriately named, in the days gone by, because through this gateway of water, vessels passed laden with untold wealth of gold dust, taken from the mines of the country bordering upon San Francisco bay.

Monterey and the Big Trees.

Doubtless the most delightful and highly appreciated, as well as the most largely patronized of all the San Francisco side trips, was the one to Monterey, Santa Cruz and the Big Trees.

It was the pleasure of the writer to escort a party of thirty-two New Jersey people on this trip. Supplied with an order from the manager of the Monterey division, which gave us special rates, we assembled at the Third Street Station in time for the 9:15 train, Saturday morning, July 10.

After a pleasant ride of about an hour, we reached Palo Alto, the site of the famous Leland Stanford, Jr., University, and were able to catch glimpses of the buildings across a beautiful park and through splendid trees, but the train speeds on and we turn away our reluctant eyes, only to be surprised and delighted by the sights of vast orchards of peaches, pears, plums, apricots and other fruits that thrive in this favored region.

We did not need to be told we were nearing San Jose, situated in one of the most charming and fruitful valleys of the world.

As the train stopped a few moments here, one of the tourists thought it a good thing to get his dinner. Seating himself placidly at the dining table, he was quietly enjoying his soup, but at the same time keeping watch of a conductor eating nearest him.

Some good spirit prompted him to say facetiously to the conductor: "No danger of my getting left while you are here." "Where are you going?" was the response. "To Del Monte," he replied. Imagine his surprise at the answer: "I am conductor of a freight train; yonder goes your train." And turning he saw it slowly leaving. With haste he paid for his dinner, and just reached the rear platform. Moral; don't keep your eye on the conductor, but on your train.

The heat in the valley was greater than we had yet experienced, and it was easy to tell when we were once more approaching the ocean, even if we had not been able to see, as it became rapidly cooler.

A most welcome sound greeted our ears about 1 P. M. It was "Del Monte!" We stepped on the platform and gazed around in bewilderment. The undreamed of loveliness on every side, reminded one of what must have been the charm of that perfect garden so many centuries ago.

Deciding to walk to the hotel, we entered a winding path leading in and out among palms and trees and flowers. We were told it was a five minute walk to the hotel, but no sign of it could be seen. Suddenly as we make a quick turn, straight before us we see a great building seemingly of interminable length, with numerous wings and branches, until one could scarcely tell where it began or ended.

After registering we passed down its long, winding corridor to our rooms. The dining room seats 500 guests. After lunch we make ready for the famous seventeen mile drive; now lengthened to nineteen.

For a mile we pass through a winding, shaded drive, then into Old Monterey, bearing on every side traces of its Spanish history. Ancient, antiquated buildings, dark eyed maidens, slow moving men.

Past the old custom house and whaling station, through Pacific Grove, on by the Chinese fishing village, and then with a turn we are in the heart of the ancient forests. Twisted oaks of grotesque form, tall towering pines; verdant and ever beautiful cypress trees, and hanging mosses with the ever varying landscape, now a climbing hill, now a quiet, sheltered valley and sparkling brook, constitute a scene that must charm the memory while life shall last.

As easily as moves the fleecy cloud, so come we by gentle transition, until, without warning, but yet not unexpectedly, where the wide sweep of water proclaimed the beautiful Pacific. On its shores we gathered beautiful abalona shells, and watched the sportive sea lion playing among the tangled sea weed. As we turn homeward by another road, we pass along an arm of the sea, after a steep climb. On our left may be seen a small herd of buffalo, while away to the right the deep blue ocean spreads in sun tinted beauty, only to be lost in a massive bank of white clouds and vapor, on whose crest the golden light of the setting sun has imprinted a rosy kiss.

Exclamations of delight fall from every lip.

By babbling brooks, up high hills, down steep slopes, we enter once more Monterey, passing by the famous and ancient and moss covered San Carlos Mission, and then in the gathering twilight, with hearts all aglow over memories of the world's finest drive, we are ready for dinner at Del Monte. I might tell of the gem of the lake so near the hotel, or of Arizona Garden, or of the intricacies of the maze, where on scarcely a half acre of ground, people may be, and sometimes are, lost, but both space and power fail me.

If you will take a long stride with me, you will find yourself in the quaint, old town of Santa Cruz. A map will show you the town of Santa Cruz, situated at the extreme southwestern point on the northern coast of the bay of Monterey. The beach on the south or bay side, calm and peaceful, that on the west or ocean side, high, rocky and dangerous, with tumultous waves that keep thundering into and through the rocks where countless ages of constant beating have worn great fissures and wide tunnels.

Though the air is calm, yet the force of the waves often causes the very rocks to tremble.

Sabbath evening found most of us in the quiet little Congregational Church, yielding to the spirit of repose and rest and worship.

An early breakfast and a dip in the invigorating but icy waters of the bay, refreshed several of those who had the courage to attempt such things.

It is no marvel to me now that most people patronize the warm, salt water baths of the pavilions, instead of the sea itself.

Nine-fifty finds us on the narrow gauge, ready for our climb of seven miles to the big trees. Those who have thus passed up the San Lorenzo valley, will not need to be reminded of the deep valley far below, seen through the beautiful foliage of stately redwoods, nor of the hills yet far above us, nor of the perfect blending of hill and valley, of tree and shrub and flower, and permeating all is the pure, clear air of that fair land, where the dreams of other countries are real and tangible. Soon we hear the brakeman's voice, "Big Tree Grove." No second call is needful. Out of the car, down the steps, through a high gate, across a wood yard we go, until halted by the shell of a monstrous tree. Within its cavernous depths fifty people can stand. The dream of our childhood is realized; we have seen the big trees. After ordering dinner for thirty-two, we secure a guide and proceed to make the tour of the grounds. The Monarch attracts our attention, then the Giant, greatest of all the single trees in the grove, being 20 feet in diameter; but space forbids my saying more than to mention the three trees 90 feet around before they divide; the fallen tree lying undecayed for ages; the single giants, the families of colossal brothers and sisters must be omitted.

Returning to the dining room we found a rapacious landlord had sold our dinner to late comers, and we could feast on nature's marvels. However, it is not good to eat over-much when travelling. With regret we leave this grand park of nature's own planting, and once more turn city ward. How we ridiculed the fairy tales of cool California as we ride along the Los Gato valley, with the thermometer more than 100 in the shade. Past large vineyards, again through great orchards, once more through San Jose, then to Alameda Mole, and at last our three day trip ends at a little past six in the evening, as we rush supperless to Mechanic's Pavilion for the consecration meeting, and enjoyed it as only those could enjoy it whose thoughts all day have been on the greatness and goodness of God.

Yellowstone Park.

In the heart of the Rocky Mountains, upon the crest of the continent, covering more than three thousand square miles of wooded slopes and weird plateaus, is Nature's wonderland, Yellowstone National Park.

How lavishly has the hand of the Creator bestowed upon this region the marvels of His power. We stand breathless before the mighty manifestations of His majesty. We are amazed at the diversity of the phenomena. Nature in her sterner mood holds revel here in steaming springs and gushing geysers, in frowning cliffs and thrilling canons, in rock-bound lakes and rushing rivers, in plunging cataracts and snow-clad mountains; yet over all, she casts a mantle of her choicest blossoms, among which the fearless, wild creatures of the wood innocently sport.

That we might behold these wonders, about seventy of our New Jersey party left their cars one afternoon at Cinnabar, the terminus of the railroad leading to the Park, and took coaches for the eagerly anticipated trip, scheduled to include five and a half days. Tourists are driven a certain number of miles each day, resting over night at well-appointed hotels, nestling in the midst of this wild, yet charming scenery. Pauses are made for lunch at convenient stations, and at all points of particular attraction. The roads are constructed by the government and, though often winding along the edge of a precipice, are smooth and safe. Driving at an altitude exceeding seven thousand feet is an exhilaration, a physical and mental tonic. The air was delightfully cool, but strongly alkaline. An annoyance scarcely expected to have been encountered here was mosquitoes of larger size and fiercer bite than the much-berated Jersey nuisance. Though smarting under their warm attentions, yet we quite rejoiced that our little state need not bear the reproach of being their only habitat, but that it shared one thing in common with this wondrous mountain land.

A drive of eight miles brought us to Mammoth Hot Springs, where ascending clouds of steam made us to realize that we had entered the realm of the thermal king, who poured his hot breath into the air. Before us were beautiful terraces, rosy, white and amber, down whose corrugated sides trickled the warm mineral waters from overflowing basins above, tier upon tier. We climbed to the summit of the lime-formed terraced hill, and looked down into the bubbling, boiling springs, whose circular margins are tinged with the most vivid coloring.

At Fort Yellowstone, is a United States cavalry post. It is the duty of the post to protect the Park from vandalism, to see that no formations are injured, nor specimens removed, and that game is unmolested. Soldiers were omnipresent. They haunted our footsteps, they rode by our side mile after mile; they galloped up in the most unexpected places. We found them always courteous, but we could not escape the consciousness of being always watched.

After a night at the comfortable Mammoth Hot Springs Hotel (fain would we have longer tarried), our party filled the waiting coaches, each drawn by four sturdy horses, and dashed southward. Owing to the unusual amount of travel this summer, farmers from the surround-

NEW JERSEY TO CALIFORNIA, '97. 93

ing country had been impressed into the Park service, consequently our conveyances were not all of the conventional type. This diversity added a spice to our experience, which the participants can appreciate.

One of the most picturesque passes is Golden Gate. The Gardiner River forces its way between precipitous rocky walls, covered in patches with yellow lichen. Following the course of the winding stream, hewn from the perpendicular cliff, for several yards suspended over the current, is constructed the wonderful roadway. Rustic Falls, leaping from a moss-covered ledge, adds its charm to the rugged scene.

Having crossed a mountain prairie, hemmed in by snow-capped peaks, and tasted the water from a natural apollinaris spring, we found ourselves beneath the bald escarpment of Obsidian Cliff. This is a mineral glass, jet black and glistening. The road here is said to have been made possible by building large fires against the rocks and shattering them by dashing cold water upon the heated portion.

At Norris Basin we stopped for lunch with the volatile Larry Mathews, and which of us shall forget his loquacity as he served our needs?

There we had our first view of a geyser. It was a small one, only the little Constant, having an interval of fifty seconds. The Black Growler, with its continuous rumbling and swift emission of volumes of hot vapor from its blackened throat, was the most direct messenger we had yet seen from the abode of the heat king. The Devil's Inkstand exhibits an angry ebullition every fifteen minutes, and then subsides far down a dark cleft. The Prince of Evil has evidently taken up extensive claims in Yellowstone. There is located his kitchen, various utensils and parts of his anatomy. The hot expulsions and sulphurous fumes are certainly suggestive of his domain. Escaping steam hedges the pathway, and one must be wary that he tread not in treacherous places.

The afternoon's drive led us near Gibbon Falls and numerous brilliantly tinted fuming springs—sulphur, emerald, sapphire and beryl. During the day we had passed through four July snow squalls—quite a unique experience. Soon after fording a fork of the Firehole River, we drew up at the Fountain Hotel.

Here is the Fountain Geyser, and not far away the Great Fountain. Immediately after our arrival, we witnessed an eruption of the latter. During a period of twenty minutes, amid a dense shroud of steam, volumes of water were again and again hurled one hundred feet in mid-air. Down the smooth terraced basin the descending deluge poured, and we were surrounded by it. The display of the Fountain, though not exceeding fifty feet, is very massive and grand.

The Mammoth Paint Pots are fascinating. A large basin and a fringe of sun-baked cones, contain exquisitely tinted clay, sluggishly boiling. Great globular bubbles burst into fragments, and smaller ones dance in curious forms all over the surface.

Near the hotel, we saw bears from the forest pillaging the open space for food.

Two nights were spent at the Fountain. During the intervening day we drove to the middle and upper geyser basins and returned. At the former are located the Excelsior, now in a state of lethargy; Turquois Spring, and Prismatic Lake, which exhibits from its margin outward all the hues of the rainbow.

At the Upper Basin, within an area scarcely exceeding a square mile, drained by the Firehole River, are the mightiest geysers of the world. The ground is covered with a grayish white deposit, over which are scattered pools and geyserite cones, some several feet high. There is the curious Grotto,—well named indeed,—the Giant, the Giantess, the Beehive, and the magnificent Castle with its neighboring well! We longed to see them play. Some gratified us, others disdainfully refused. We turned to Old Faithful, dear reliable geyser, amid so many erratic ones. We knew when to expect Old Faithful; he never disappoints. His interval is now seventy-four minutes. As the time approached, the steam increased, and the basin having filled, the water was ejected in spasmodic spurts. At the appointed instant, a huge watery pillar lifted itself one hundred and fifty feet and stood nearly four minutes throbbing and pulsing. It was awful. It was grand. After it had subsided, at the risk of a foot scalding in the bowl-like depressions, we peered down its rusty throat; but it told no tale.

At will we wandered for hours among these strange outlets of the subterranean world. The Cascade, Grotto, Economic, Oblong and Riverside were in action. The Riverside, attaining a height of one hundred feet, spurts obliquely, and its discharge falls directly into the river. Many are the pools and geysers, each with a particular charm! Morning Glory Spring is a perfect gem. How weird it all is! What a fierce force has here rifted the earth to its heated core, and yet keeps open the channels of communication through which these majestic tokens of the power below are being hurled!

Our next day's drive led us over the continental divide, and near Keppler's Cascades, a series of enchanting falls. During the morning a beautiful elk with uplifted horns appeared at the road-side, and stood gazing at us with his soft, dark eyes. Hunting being forbidden, the shyest creature knows no fear. Chipmunks frisk like kittens at the forest's edge.

At noon we reached Yellowstone Lake, nearly eight thousand feet above sea level, closely clasped by rugged mountains, among which the blue waters reach their shining arms. The lake is swarming with trout. Hot Springs Cone, a few yards from the shore, offers peculiar advantages to the fisherman. It is a flat rock with a boiling spring in the centre. Here one may stand, catch a fish, and without disengaging it from the hook, plunge it into the spring, cooking it in less than two minutes.

At West Thumb Bay our party divided, about half taking boat across the lake to the hotel at the outlet, and the remainder driving along the charming shore.

From the Lake Hotel next morning, we followed the Yellowstone River to the canon, pausing at the mud volcano. What a hideous, yet fascinating object is this! From the bottom of a deep mouth-like crater, with overarching lip, is belched a rumbling, sickening mass of lead-colored mud. The force not being sufficient to expel the pasty upheaval beyond the outer rim, it falls back, and the monster is obliged to re-swallow it.

At noon we came to the canon. We paused at the Upper Falls and admired their graceful beauty. For several hours we were permitted to view the majesty of nature, grander than imagination had ever pictured. In that glorious, natural temple, speech was almost sacrilege. We stood in the presence of God's sublime handiwork. At the brink of the Lower Falls, the fullness of view was first revealed. The river, transparent as crystal, in an instant powerfully plunges over the precipice three hundred and sixty feet. It descends like a massive drapery in long, snow-white, effervescent folds. It leaps against the rocks below, and is shattered into the most ethereal mist, which catches the sun's spectrum, and holds it poised.

From the verge of the narrowed, foam-flecked stream, rise the canon walls to the appalling height of fifteen hundred feet, bristling with pinnacles, obelisks and turrets, sometimes supported by gigantic buttresses, sometimes thrusting out sharp ridges of rock, and again sweeping with a clear, smooth slide from crest to base. The castles along the Rhine, and the towering cathedral spires find here their loftier counterpart. And all this stupendous mass God has touched with a wealth of color which defies description. Brilliant yellows predominate, which merge into orange, terra cotta, rose and crimson. Dazzling white, lavender and creamy tints, blend with the richer hues. Far below are vivid mosses and dark evergreen forests occasionally push themselves part way down the slopes. So glorious is the scene that we seem to be standing at the portal of the infinite. As we passed from point to point of observation upon the ledge, lingering upon far-jutting crags in the heart of this mystery of beauty, at times gazing full in the face of the shimmering falls, each moment beholding a vision of more overpowering sublimity, the nobler emotions of every soul must have been deepened, and we felt that it was good to be there.

On the summits of sharp shafts below, the eagles built their nests. We could see the young within, and the parent birds winging their flight across the chasm.

Reluctantly we took the long, last look; but the exalted moments of life are not abiding, and one must descend to the commonplace, better for having received the brief inspiration.

That evening we held our wonted Christian Endeavor

service in the hotel, and hearts voiced the praise of God. To these services, men who rarely, if ever, had attended religious worship; hotel attendants, drivers and soldiers, listened with curiosity and interest.

The following was our last day in the Park. We returned to Cinnabar via Virginia Cascades, Norris, and Mammoth Hot Springs, having completed a circuit of nearly two hundred miles.

Our trip into Wonderland had drawn to a close, but it has been an epoch in our lives; it has become a part of our being; its impress upon us will never be effaced.

New Jersey C. E. Special.

It is safe to say, without boasting or exaggeration, that no C. E. delegates had a finer train to San Francisco, than that which carried the New Jersey Endeavorers and their friends. At many stations over the various railroads this was said by railroad men who were competent to judge. The Pullman Palace Car Company were very considerate of the wishes and requests of the New Jersey management and gave them the very best service possible. Especially was this so with the conductors and porters who were the very best in the Pullman Company.

It was the intention of the Transportation Committee to run only one special train, but so many applications for the transcontinental journey were received, that two full trains of seven palace cars attached, were needed to carry the Endeavorers to California. And even then one hundred and thirty-six people were left at home simply because of lack of room, the committee not being willing to take the responsibility and care of a third special train. In all, four hundred and eight-one persons were carried to San Francisco by the New Jersey C. E. Special in its two sections. This does not include the train crew or conductors and porters. There were four hunlred and eighty-one persons who had tickets. Not even the Transportation Manager was allowed to ride free. The first section had the cars Nadura, Hebrides, Sydenham, Superb, Saale, Alsace and Canton.

In the second section were the cars Burton, Utrecht, Epsom, Proteus, Keystone, Dorante and New Hampshire.

On the trip a catalogue of the party was published, which was necessarily very incomplete. It has been the desire and aim of the committee to gather up the interesting things that transpired in each car on the journey, and attach the names of the members of each car to the article. It has been very difficult to get such articles, and more difficult to get the names of individuals in each car, as all the original diagrams have been lost. But the most active and faithful efforts have produced the results that follow.

Nadura.

This musical name, although it belongs to only a Pullman car, is surrounded by very pleasant associations to the company of about forty people, who spent many days and nights under one sheltering roof. There, as the days passed, we learned to overlook the faults and see the best traits in one another's characters, more and more, till we decided among ourselves that ours was the most agreeable car on the train.

At the beginning of the journey Nadura occupied, appropriately, the first position on the train. But at St. Louis, where we backed out of the depot, like the boy in the spelling match, she had to "go down foot." This was at first considered unfortunate by some, but we soon found the absence of coal dust and the possession of a rear platform more than made amends for extra rocking. The rear platform became a favorite resort for viewing the scenery, and when we passed through the Royal Gorge, probably fifteen of our number were packed on the platform and steps, enjoying the sight.

NEW JERSEY TO CALIFORNIA, '97.

Always next to Nadura, before or behind, came Hebrides (pronounced He-brides). This being the ladies' car, an interesting feud soon arose and raged more or less violently throughout the journey. The Hebrides having made a rule that passage through that car after certain hours was prohibited, it became clearly the duty of the Nadura gentlemen to go through as often as possible. This culminated, after leaving San Francisco, in the great Battle of He-brides, spoken of elsewhere.

Nadura was, doubtless, the only car having a bride, bridegroom, and the minister who married them, all in one section. As we were provided with a physician, it was deemed best to take an undertaker also, although the latter, fortunately, found no professional use for his talents.

When we were in need of refreshments we had "Watermelon," and lest we become too frivolous, "Calamity" dwelt among us. Most of the company were provided with nicknames, but we forbear to harrow their feelings by a public announcement. The "Sportive elf" in No. 1 did much to enliven the time, while it is to be hoped that the man who feared we should miss the scenery of Pittsburgh, at an unseemly hour in the morning, will get his reward on earth.

Although Nadura had no organized band to go about serenading with combs, yet there was a great deal of unappreciated musical talent lying unheeded, perhaps, during the daytime. But to one awakening in the very early morning hours, at the time when the birds in the woods give their opening concert, what a revelation! From near the rear door, from the upper berth of No. 8, from the vestibule and various invisible sources, poured forth a snoraphic chorus, certainly unrivaled, and that, properly trained, might win lasting laurels for Nadura.

Endeavor meetings were held frequently, usually at

twilight, and the singing, too, was a source of pleasure.

Throughout the journey Nadura was the abiding place of a company of people, friendly, courteous and congenial (except on the subject of early rising) and all will place the many enjoyable experiences here among the choice "Pictures that hang on Memory's Wall."

Adams, Annie M., Atlantic City.
Adams, Carrie E., Atlantic City.
Aumack, G., Keyport.
Bell, E. S., Atlantic City.
Bell, Mrs. E. S., Atlantic City.
Clark, Aaron L., Bridgeton.
Compton, Charles W., Newark.
Cosman, Miss M. A., Vineland.
Currey, Miss, Weehawken.
Currey, Miss J. S., Weehawken.
Cummins, R., Washington.
Dalrymple, Aaron, Washington.
Dawes, Theodore B., Washington.
Dawes, Mrs. Theodore B., Washington.
Davis, W. H., M. D., East Orange.
Duerkes, Miss, Weehawken.
Exton, Emma, Trenton.
Fitzer, J. R., Salem.
Gaskill, Florence, Mt. Holly.
Graff, Lewis E., Haddonfield.
Hoagland, Rev. Charles H., Asbury.
Hendrick, Miss S. E., Newark.
Irving, Rev. D. O., East Orange.
Kaighn, Richard C., Ellisburg.
Koehler, Andrew G., Somerville.
Lawshe, David, Trenton.
Leuly, Emil, Hoboken.
Mattison, Mrs. Jennie E., Newark.
Mulford, Fannie, Millville.
Murray, Miss M., King of Prussia, Pa.
Owens, Mrs. Wesley R., Trenton.
Page, Mrs. O., Newark.
Painter, Annie, New Brunswick.
Palmer, Mrs. Imogene, Atlantic City.
Roe, H. Estelle, Rutherford.
Robinson, William T., Freehold.
Rumbarger, Miss M., Atlantic City.
Smith, Elizabeth J., Branchville.
Stegeman, John F., Newark.
Sinkinson, Rev. C. D., Atlantic City.
Terhune, Rev. J. A., Hughsonville, N. Y.
Terhune, Mrs. J. A., Hughsonville, N. Y.
Thompson, William W., Freehold.
Weller, Lizzie, Washington.
Wright, Mrs. Mary E., Atlantic City.

Hebrides.

The Hebrides was inhabited by forty-six ladies, some young, some old, some "fair, fat and forty;" all peace-loving; no jars (except pickle jars) but perfect harmony. One lady on being told that she would travel in this car, said:

"The idea of being all that time with a lot of women—all cranks." Now, she is one of the loudest in praise of the life among them. Another declared the millenium had come, or it would have been impossible for so many women to live in such peace for twenty days.

The days were spent in viewing the magnificent scenery, comparing notes, giving impromptu entertainments and luncheons, and last, but in no wise least, writing poetry. A paper called "The Hebrides Herald" was edited, showing up the conduct of certain men from neighboring cars. These men affected the fear of entering the "He-brides," as they were fond of calling our home, but in reality, nothing pleased them better than to come in and share our good times; the fame of which had spread through the whole train.

The crowning hour, however, was when the curtains of night were slowly gathering. The desperate efforts of our porter to "make down" the beds, the untiring "cake walk" from berth to dressing room, to and fro, the screams and scrambles following the warning cry, "Man coming," the struggles with the stepladder, and the sighs of those who mounted them, the sorrows of hair-dressing, and the innate perniciousness of hair-pins, the swaying car and the plunging bags, all combined to produce a scene unrivaled, except by the "streets of Cairo."

After a succession of these day and night scenes, the last day came—that day—especially freighted with pleasant memories. Many expressions of good will and congratulations on being a "He-bride," greeted us on every side, and we left our associates with the hope that each had made a little "sunshine" along our route to the "Golden Gate" and return.

Bross, Mrs. S. B., Newark.
Bross, Marion, Newark.
Benche, Anna S., Hyde Park.
Bauer, A. Mame, Jersey City.
Brown, M. Florence, Newark.
Borden, Rachel B., Monroeville.
Borden, Fannie C., Jacobstown.
Bradley, Mary I., Lee, Mass.
Catlin, Sarah F., Brooklyn.
Catlin, Miss H. A., Brooklyn.
Coe, Jessie D., Nutley.
Crissman, Ellen G., Branchville.
Crissman, Mattie, Branchville.
Condit, Mrs. M. B., Orange Valley.
Coe, Caroline M., Newark.
Craig, Mrs. R. F., New Germantown.
Durling, Josie, Hackettstown.
Ennis, Mrs. E. B., Newark.
Fisher, Betty, Jersey City.
Hammond, Julia M., Closter.
Hoyt, Juliette M., Hoboken.
Lutz, Rose, Trenton.
Lutz, Elizabeth, Trenton.
Martin, Annie E., Newark.
McKenzie, Annie D., Newark.
Mac Morran, Margaret, Newark.
McGarrah, Grace A., Brooklyn.
McGarrah, Agatha, Brooklyn.
Moore, Mrs. S. E., Freehold.
Moore, Estelle M., Freehold.
Moore, Mrs. M., Jersey City.
Nicholson, Belle, Califon.
Platt, Sarah E., Red Bank.
Precht, Louisa, Trenton.
Park, Ada A., Jersey City.
Runyon, Sarah DeM., Millington.
Smith, Ida E., Newark.
Trimmer, M. Mildred, Middle Valley.
Tomlinson, Cora, Plainfield.
Van Alen, M. Freda, Heath, N. Y.
Van Kirk, Lizzie, Griggstown.
Valentine, Mrs. Seth, Newark.
Van Cleef, Mabel, Newark.
Woodruff, Hannah H., Bridgeton.
Woolman, Helen R., Newark.
Wade, Margaret I., Irvington.

Sydenham.

My Dear Sue.—Of course you are anxious to hear of our wonderful trip, and I will have to begin by describing our "Apartment House." The Sydenham is one of the most elegantly appointed and exclusive apartment houses. No baggage is allowed to stand in its corridors, and its janitor and head steward, Ben by name, took special delight in keeping it always clean and bright, and was ever careful and watchful of his own.

One day a porter from a nearby hotel, "The Superb," wishing to find Ben, rang the call bell of No. 6 in a very energetic and persistent manner; when Ben appeared, he remarked, in a very unconcerned way: "I knew that wasn't any white ring." Our flats, all delightful for location, were only rented to small families, and we proved a most con-

NEW JERSEY TO CALIFORNIA, '97.

genial household. The proprietor and general manager, Rev. T. E. Davis and wife occupied a central one, and very often Mr. D. insisted on going to another for his own. They sometimes took boarders, but owing to the office being there, and people constantly wanting to see him on all sorts of business, they were rather crowded at times. You know those nice people, the Dyott's? Well, for a time they had to be separated, and lodged in different flats, till one was vacated, when they took possession.

We had a home restaurant and lunch room in No. 5, kept by the Batemans, who were most obliging sort of people and set a fine table. Two ladies from No. 1 took their meals with them, but had our trip lasted much longer, doubtless they would have had to provide meals at home, as they had a couple of very attentive visitors,—one being a foxy sort of chap, it was hard to know just what he did want, but Miss Ribble knows he likes buttermilk; the other apparently is very fond of the good things of life, but a certain young lady may prefer DuBois to avoirdupois.

The ladies in No. 3, each owned a "blickie," and hailed with delight the sight of a cow, or "Pure Milk for Sale." A milk diet certainly agrees with Miss Porter. The flat occupied by the Harris family had a reception room and private balcony; they were wise in their choice, else Miss Bertie never could have entertained her numerous admirers, still the poor girl had the bad luck to lose a bran new sailor hat, just when it was impossible for one or all to give chase. As a rule, we were very quiet and decorous after the lights were low, but sometimes the ladies in Flat E were disturbed by most "payneful" snores.

On our journey we came nigh unto a village called Hebrides, absolutely under petticoat government, with the one exception of the "Board of Public Works." As we were near to them some little time; they, wishing to be friendly and acquaint us with the doings of the inhabitants, sent us a copy of their "Herald," giving full particulars of a recent midnight raid on the poor lone females. Appreciating their kind friendliness, three of our bright minds were appointed to draw up and send these Hebrides a fitting set of resolutions, which was done with all proper form and ceremony. Then knowing the ability of our household and recognizing the fact that a great deal of musical talent was wasting its sweetness on the desert air, we engaged, as leader, Signor Dungan, and formed the new popular comb orchestra. Who knows? you may hear us East this Winter. First we gave a concert to our friends, the Hebrides, thereby gaining local reputation, so that we had to make a tour of the neighboring towns. Where we could be appreciated, we were received with joy and gladness, but one evening, arrayed in fitting (?) white garments, we travelled to a remote village, only to find on our way home the gates of another town, through which we had to pass, locked against us. They must have been frightened at our very appearance, for women rose screaming from their beds, the life of our leader was threatened, and we were glad to reach the Sydenham in safety.

Quite a different experience was that of Mt. Siskiyou, on July 14th, when some of us were presented with bouquets of beautiful flowers, and twisted among the stems, some found addresses, or a tender billetdoux from their Mt. gallants.

"Live and Learn"—At Colorado Springs one of our number, a Mrs. Wood from New bubrgh, N. Y., was taught the difference between pennies and nickels. She paid her trolley fare in pennies, and was amazed to see the conductor, after looking contemptuously at them a minute, throw them against the stones by the wayside, remarking as he did so: "I never take such stuff." On the afternoon of July 22, our large assembly room was full to overflowing with the Snides and their guests, to listen to Miss Catlin, the famous elocutionist of Morristown, N. J. She gave a most pleasing entertainment, and was followed by the talented minstrel Harvey, who sang for us.

I've written yards already and must stop, but I wish I had time to tell you of the meetings we attended along the route, for the Sydenham was always well represented; of the wheel Miss Voorhees borrowed without permission of the owner, and her painful reflections the next day; of the uneasy slumbers of some of our people that last night, all on account of the cracker crumbs, feather dusters, dust pans, etc., being in beds, and stockings, instead of in their proper places, and of others of our household who enjoyed the trip, but have not become famous thereby, but I must close. Very Sincerely. M.

Bateman, C. H., Somerville.
Bateman, Mrs. C. H., Somerville.
Conover, Mrs. A. E., Asbury Park.
Cook, Jessie M., Bound Brook.
Davis, Rev. T. E., Bound Brook.
Davis, Mrs. T. E., Bound Brook.
Dorsett, Edna, Yonkers, N. Y.
DuBois, Mary E., Freehold.
Dunham, Elfieda M., Bound Brook.
Dyott, Rev. L. R., Newark.
Dyott, Mrs. L. R., Newark.
Egbert, Rose M., Nyack, N. Y.
Harris, Henrietta T., Belvidere.
Harris, Roberta R., Belvidere.
Hickman, Mary B., Bound Brook.
Leigh, Mabel, Somerville.
Osborn, Laura, Peekskill, N. Y.
Payne, H. G., Red Bank.
Payne, Mrs. H. G., Red Bank.
Porter, Amelia, Somerville.
Ribble, Anna O., East Millstone.
Rockafellow, Alice, Bound Brook.
Rogers, Josie A., New Brunswick.
Smock, Mrs. R. P., Asbury Park.
Tappen, Addie, Bound Brook.
Voorhees, Ada G., Somerville.
White, Elizabeth, Passaic.
Wood, Mrs. Sarah S., Newburg. N. Y.

Superb.

There is one morning in the year ninety-seven indelibly stamped on the memories of the four hundred and eighty-one, who began their trip across the continent, not the dark continent but our own surprisingly new, bright and wonderful.

The only drawing room car on the train was the Superb. The six cosy little parlors were taken possession of by twenty-one persons. Being occupants of drawing rooms, we were sympathized with as being "not in it," with the fun and good times elsewhere. Although it may have appeared that we were shut off from most of the fun prevailing; we feel that the "Superb"-ers had the "cream" of the good time, and our best wish for all is that they may cross the continent in the car "Superb."

We left Jersey City bright as the day itself, and from the moment of starting, the Stars and Stripes, our own country's flag waved in our room.

Oh, how we flew, from the far East to the far West, dipping a little to the south, and touching the extreme north of the States.

As we travelled farther away from New Jersey, we became more neighborly with each other, and before many hours had passed, were as one large family. What delightful times we had at our "Afternoon Tea" and "Luncheon," when we could entertain our friends in our own room, and there enjoy ourselves undisturbed.

One, who proved himself in many ways very necessary to the comfort of the twenty-one, our jolly, good natured, fun loving porter, George, will never be forgotten. "The key to a man's heart is through his stomach," and we were often sad, being truly hungry. Then George would gravely state that the next station would be need-more, and advise us to lay in a supply of tomatoes that we might catch-up, (we were then something short of a day behind schedule time.)

When food seemed an impossibility, George and his friend, Ben, anticipating the wants of the party, supplied all who wished with refreshing lemonade, and even hot tea and coffee. One day when business was at its best, and George was doing his utmost to supply everyone, on reaching his "kitchen," what did he see tied to the door-knob, but a dead chicken. Oh, what a shout was heard, for the unfortunate chicken had met its fate many days before, and, as George said, "Not even saltpeter could bring it back." This was a grave, solemn joke, having been performed by the clergy to the sacrifice of their high (?) collars and sober (?) influence. Ever after, this portion of the car was known as "George's Buffet."

Before reaching Salt Lake City, we were advised to lay in a supply of provisions, and this we all did while with the hospitable Mormons. Some of our companions acted upon the suggestion so well that they purchased, not only food, but chafing dish, knives, forks, etc., and were prepared for the very worst. The "very worst" never came, however, and how sumptuously these friends dined on frizzled beef, (cooked with condensed milk), fried eggs, fresh salmon and many more luxurious "tasties."

One of our most delightful memories, and one that we will recall often, was the first Sunday afternoon of train life. (We were compelled to travel this Sunday.) How we enjoyed our Sunday School class of nine members, and how kindly and graciously we were met at three o'clock by our teacher, Rev. Mr. Ottman, in his drawing room. We shall never forget our lesson of that day, and our hour was very short. It passed more quickly than any other of train life, and was brimful of "helps," not only for train life, but for our world life.

It was impossible to have any of the prayer meetings in

the "Superb," but we were always invited to attend the meetings in the neighboring cars, and accepted all such invitations with genuine pleasure.

Our trip from beginning to end was of solid comfort and enjoyment, and all of the "Superb"-ers enjoyed good health but one, and to him every one felt drawn, and missed him sadly during the days he was confined to his bed, and how everyone from all parts of the train, rejoiced when he was able to be with us again.

What a glorious trip we had; how we enjoyed being together, and how we all hope to meet again.

As we journeyed toward San Francisco, and again when homeward bound, we felt more than can be expressed. We were awed and silenced by the wonderful beauties of our own country, and, in the words of our own countryman, wish to sing:

>"O, beautiful and grand,
>My own, my native land!
>Of thee I boast;
>Great Empire of the West,
>The dearest and the best,
>Made up of all the rest,
>I love thee most."

Americanism fastens us together in loyalty, while we feel more closely drawn to each other by the blest

>"Tie that bind,
>Our hearts in mutual love."

And feel individually the truth of Rev. 4:11. "Thou art worthy, O Lord, to receive glory and honor and power; for thou hast created all things, and for Thy pleasure they are and were created."

NEW JERSEY TO CALIFORNIA, '97.

Now parted from one another, we feel more able than ever before, to sing, (as we did that eventful day on Marshall Pass),

"Praise God from whom all blessings flow,
Praise Him, all creatures here below;
Praise Him above, ye heavenly host;
Praise Father, Son and Holy Ghost."

Aumack, Theodore, Freehold.
Aumack, Mrs. Theodore, Freehold.
Barnett, Joanna G., Newark.
Chapman, D. D., Rev. J. W., Phila.
Dey, Lurena, Newark.
Duncan, Lucy G., Newark.
Kennard, Jessie A., Brooklyn.
Ketcham, Alice E., Hoboken.
Ketcham, Edith A., Hoboken.
Keasbey, Edward, Perth Amboy.
Keasbey, Mrs. Edward, Perth Amboy.
Kirk, Mrs. Rachel, Newark.
Monroe, Miss M. L., Southport, Conn.
Newkirk, Mrs. Margaret, Brooklyn.
Ottman, Rev. Ford C., Newark.
Shepherd, O. L., Freehold.
Shepherd, Mrs. O. L., Freehold.
Taylor, Mrs. W. H., Charleston, S. C.
Taylor, Elizabeth M., Charleston, S. C.
Valentine, Mrs. E. B., Brooklyn.
Wrigley, Jennie, Newark.

Saale.

I am a comfortable, well-built Pullman car, and though I boast no state rooms, I offer pleasant accommodations.

When I was attached to the New Jersey Special, I found myself filled with people who were anticipating Yellowstone Park. They were genial people of all ages; not many Endeavorers. William, my stalwart porter, always kept me in good order.

It was a source of amusement to hear the discussions concerning the pronunciation of my name. Commonly, I was called Sally.

Everything flowed smoothly until the night we lay at Manitou. Well do I remember the excitement which there stirred by occupants, when five tickets for Pike's Peak were brought in to satisfy fourteen claimants. Waves of disappointment selfishness and renunciation, swept over me from end to end.

On Sunday morning in Utah, I listened to Mr. Chapman's sweet words, and Christian Endeavor services were frequently held within my walls.

Starting on my return trip from California, I missed many familiar faces, among them two cordial committeemen and my portly friend from the smoker. New ones, however, filled the vacancies, and they formed a pleasant company.

There were one or two flirtations, or serious attachments, (who can tell?) that I watched with interest.

At Portland, I found myself alone with the Burton, and our young people became acquainted, growing quite sociable; then how forlorn we deserted cars felt while our inmates were coaching through Yellowstone!

Some of our lads and lasses had a gay frolic at St. Paul. They were pining for ice cream, and when we reached there late Saturday evning, two good hearted young men set out to get it. How I laughed to see them tugging in a huge freezer, with three gallons of cream and bags of cakes and pears, all for twelve dainty eaters! How the borrowed plates and spoons flourished, and how the cream disappeared, notwithstanding its bulk.

At length my trip came to a close. As I crossed the Delaware, I heard a promising youth gladly shout, "O, Jersey, we're coming, we're coming, Jersey, I love you best of all."

Ballinger, Levi, Moorestown.
Ballinger, Mrs. Levi, Moorestown.
Budd, Avorene L., Mt. Holly.
Burgess, Agnes E., Inwood, N. Y.
Compton, Charles W., Newark.
Campbell, Mrs. Mary, Camden.
Davy, Sarah M., Orange.
Dickinson, C. C., Camden.
Dickinson, Mrs. C. C., Camden.
Engle, Mrs., Mt. Holly.
Ehni, Christopher, Raritan.
Ehni, Edward C., Raritan.
Gulick, Walter A., Camden.
Hitchner, F. G., Camden.
Humphrey, M. D., Edw., Somerton, Pa.
Kenyon, J. C., Raritan.

Long, Agnes H., Philadelphia.
Lindsley, Miss L. M., Orange.
Lindsley, Emma L., Orange.
Lumbar, Rev. W. T. S., Moorestown.
Lumbar, Mrs. W. T. S., Moorestown.
Marks, Mrs. L., Orange.
Martin, Nellie, Rahway.
Mason, Mary L., Haddonfield.
Miller, R. Anna, Somerville.
Montgomery, Mr., Pemberton.
Norcross, Mrs. Annie, Mt. Holly.
Prall, Minnie, Philadelphia.
Rogers, J. J., Medford.
Roy, Anna C., Inwood, N. Y.
Sanborn, Mrs. George W., Somerville.
Shaffer, Ada L., Hackensack.
Shaffer, Lulu R., Hackensack.
Warne, Rev. D. R., Kingston.
Warne, Mrs. D. R., Kingston.
West, Samuel, Riverton.
West, Mrs. Samuel, Riverton.
Woodhouse, Mrs. E., Moorestown.

Alsace.

We come now to the people who were denominated "All-sassy," a title having its derivation and root in the word Alsace (al-zas). It was not that they were more impudent than their fellow travellers that they were thus styled, for they were quiet and unobtrusive, content with themselves and their surroundings, but because they occupied the Alsace, or the best car in the train.

The Alsace contained the youth and the age, those that were married and those that wanted to be; those that had brought their dear ones with them, and one that had left his sweetheart behind. Of this last named we have a melancholy tale to unfold. When our train pulled out of Jersey City, Tommy's sweetheart stood upon the platform with tears in her eyes, pleading "Don't you go Tommy, don't go." But Tommy was resolute, and with a joyous exterior, but with heart-burnings within, he sped away to the far West. As the distance increased, and Tommy's chances of caressing his sweetheart on the next Sunday night, grew rapidly less, Tommy's spirits drooped correspondingly, and when Colorado Springs was reached his thermostat showed the zero mark, and Tommy vowed he had all the enchantment he wanted, and he did not care about continuing the view at such long range. Resolved never to leave her again, with lightened heart he chartered the fast express to carry him back to the girl he left behind on the plains of Hoboken; and Tommy was with us no more.

One of the sections in this car was occupied by two bright and vivacious ladies who had never pledged allegiance to any man, and a gentleman—a stranger to the ladies. His advent into their presence at the beginning of the journey was destined to free their minds of all doubts concerning his ability to make two hearts beat as one, provided another heart could be found that would keep time with his.

After depositing his traps and settling himself comfortably in his seat he opened the conversation with the declaration somewhat amusing to the ladies, "I am a widower." Whether the gentleman deemed the statement necessary to his then present safety or future happiness, the ladies were unable to determine, but judging from the attention which he from that time commanded, some of the wise ones afterwards concluded that Bro. Jackson possessed considerable sagacity. Thenceforth sister Brown and aunt Fanny vied with each other in making brother Jackson's trip all that could be desired, and when we left Livingston it was supposed the climax had been reached, and that sister Brown had been left at the quarter pole in the race, for brother Jackson's heart-strings. He and aunt Fanny were missing, and all concluded that an elopement had taken place. Good mother Conklin declared that she had seen it all the time, and thus we all were led to commiserate sister Brown. Condolence continued to be poured in upon her until we had almost reached Cinnabar, when brother Jackson, smiling and blushing like a new blown rose, appeared to spoil the fun, and we learned that aunt Fanny had simply been left behind, and the romance which he had fancied was shattered.

This car boasted the only poetic porter on the train. Toward the close of the journey he set his muse going and evolved the following:

* "Mr. Davis, he would wait for you, but he'd be losing time;
He has got to make connection on the B. & O. R. R. line;
The engineer, he was ready; he blew his whistle, too;
He said he was going to drive this train, and drive it right straight through.

"Young man, young man, you're too late for this train;
Young man, young man, Mr. Davis is not to blame;
Young man, young man, you're too late for this train;
Another section is on behind, for this is a New Jersey train.

"Some says the New York Central made the fastest time;
I'll tell you about a road out West—I'll tell what she done:
She left Kansas City sharp, at half-past one;
She arrived in Denver, Colorado, by the setting of the sun.

"Mr. Wagner says to Pullman, 'I'll tell you what I'll do,
You give me the Michigan Central, and you take the C. B. & Q.'
Mr. Pullman says to Mr. Wagner, 'Ill bet you you what I'll do,
If you don't pay me lots of money I'll take off my vestibule.'"

While waiting at Ogden three members of the party strolled through the streets of the city. They met and engaged in conversation a resident, and during the conversation he proposed that he be allowed to procure a team and carriage and show the party the points of interest about the city. The proposal was cheerfully acceded to, and they were driven about the city, through the adjoining country, about seven miles into Ogden Canon, which pre-

*Note—A young man was left behind at St. Paul and this gave occasion for these lines.

sented one of the prettiest views and scenes of the entire trip. There was seen Bridal Veil Falls, a beautiful sheet of water falling over a high precipice, and the Ogden City Water Works, one of the largest in the world. One of the most pleasing features of this delightful side trip was the modest and unassuming manner of this Ogden City resident who, it was learned, not from himself, but from another, was Mr. H. H. Spencer, the Mayor of the city. This incident is mentioned as an illustration of western hospitality.

While our train lay at Ogden a bevy of small girls with inquiring minds, and, as we afterwards learned, very intelligent, came into our car to see the porter make up the berths or "beds," as the girls called them. Their running fire of questions and conversation with the occupants of the car showed them to be very well informed concerning their Mormon religion, and one of the girls in expressing her amazement at the opinions entertained by the Eastern people concerning the Mormons said, "the Eastern folks come out here expecting to find us with horns and hoofs."

Altogether ours was a happy, pleasure seeking company, enjoying all about us; our hearts made lighter at times by the refrain which came floating from the drawing room, "Don't you care," and we didn't.

Blakely, Agnes M., White Plains, N. Y.
Brookfield, Mrs. C. M., Newark.
Brown, Addie, Camden.
Conkling, Mrs. Oscar, Basking Ridge.
Conkling, Florence, Basking Ridge.
Cattell, Frances V., Philadelphia.
Crane, Anna M., Newark.
Crane, Mrs. Sarah F., Newark.
Dessart, Victor E., Arlington.
Dessart, Mrs. Victor E., Arlington.
Earl, Elizabeth, Elizabeth.
Flanagan, Alice, Philadelphia.
Gabel, Mary, Philadelphia.
Geissele, Hilda T., Newark.
Gibson, Fred., Arlington.
Gilmor, Rev. J. S., Congers, N. Y.
Gilmor, Mrs. J. S., Congers, N, Y.
Hepburn, Mrs. W. H., White Plains, N. Y.
Jackson, Thomas, Ocean Grove.
Kennard, Edward, Brooklyn.
Levy, C. B., Freehold.
La Bar, L. T., Beattystown.
La Bar, Mrs. L. T., Beattystown.

McClellan, Douglas Y., West Hoboken.
Pierpont, Caroline L., West Hoboken.
Pierpont, Ella V. C., West Hoboken.
Smith, Thomas F., N. Y. City.
Taylor, W. W., Holmdel.
Taylor, Mrs. W. W., Holmdel.
Wainwright, Halstead H., Manasquan.
Wainwright, Mrs. Halstead, Manasquan.

Canton.

Among the many thousands of persons in the great exodus to California this year, were twenty-nine characteristic individuals on the car "Canton."

With us were lawyers, doctors, teachers, church officials, young men and maidens, all of whom were bent on having a good time. We will not soon forget those last good byes on the 28th day of June, those heart-felt sympathies of our best friends, and the tears so freely shed by not a few of our party. But soon we bade "farewell to every fear and wiped our weeping eyes." Once fairly settled in our beautiful car the work of getting acquainted with the many strangers was soon begun, for we were to spend nearly eleven days in crossing the continent together. At first we sat in our respective sections like so many soldiers in a line, waiting for an opportunity to break the first law of etiquette, and share our feelings with our strange neighbors. In this rather unpleasant time of suspense, our car was hastened through the tunnels on the Baltimore & Ohio Railroad, and passed the Washington Monument as if there was nothing at all worth seeing in this Eastern country.

Scarcely had we started on our way up the historic Potomac, when the delicious aroma of coffee made a strong appeal to our olfactory sense.

A glance down the aisle of the car revealed the fact that more than one alcohol lamp, with complete culinary outfits, were in possession of a skillful maidens. This was a familiar scene three times a day, and the generosity of our kind lady friends will be remembered long after much of the grand scenery of the wonderful Rockies has faded from our memories. On the first morning of our trip the cause of woman's rights was settled. The ladies discovered that seven men had a dressing room seven times as large as the one used by twenty-two women. The majority ruled in our small Republic, and both men and women afterward made their toilet in the spacious smoker, with a freedom that would amaze our fastidious old maids of the East. Our ladies rejoiced that they were not "He-brides," that is passengers on the car Hebrides, where there was no man except the colored porter, or Brigham Young, as he was styled. The three married men of our party were very useful to the young ladies and gentlemen, for two days had not passed before every one in the car knew that our young Camden lawyer was fast becoming a Croesus, and that our embryo doctor of Moorestown gave promise of a brilliant future. We were a happy people, noting familiar flowers and birds, and comparing notes about rare bits of scenery which especially struck our fancy. But when the promised rides through the city of St. Louis were lost in the shades of night, and we had to endure six hours wait at Kansas City in a tropical temperature, which prostrated men and women, our legal talent was up in arms and declared there was ("cause for action.") But "every rose has its thorn," and an ideal ride across the Kansas prairie, and a trip up Pike's Peak were sufficient to arouse the most sanguine heart, and never again was the voice of a "kicker" heard on the "Canton." On the whole, our car gave our kind manager, Mr. Davis, very little cause for worry. We could entertain ourselves when nature did not appeal to our senses, and the intricate questions of theology, psychology, sociology and matrimony were discussed with a skill that would astonish our college fraternity. Deafening shouts of laughter were daily heard in the smoker, or some corner of the car where were nestled a group of "jokers." We had a number of excellent story tellers, but one of our party was especially gifted. He never ran out of jokes, and often related a story as old as Methuselah, with a freshness that provoked applause from the admiring audience. Many of our stories had an appropriate setting in the surrounding scenery. While crossing the desert our train halted, which was a rare thing to do!

There was little to look at except alkali plains, covered with sage bush. While waiting, our joker observed a lank good-for-nothing looking fellow leaning against the station, and he inquired of the stranger the distance to the next stop? The slouchy man of the desert answered in a low, husky voice, "three miles." Our joker asked what malady caused his weakness, and he replied, "the land was so poor he could not raise his voice!" At Helper, Utah, our train (strange to say) had to rest several hours. It was a beautiful Sunday morning, and the little desert town labored manfully to satisfy the hunger of more than a thousand Christian Endeavorers. A number of Cantonians visited a restaurant in a vain search for food, until finally one of our number pitifully asked the charming matron if she would be so kind as to give a poor starving man something to eat? The hungry look and persuasive words had the desired effect, and a fine breakfast of ham and eggs was enjoyed for the small consideration of "two bits." Often a few of our party stampeded the culinary departments of restaurants and helped themselves to tea, coffee, bread, butter, etc., while hundreds, less persistent, returned to the car with aching voids. The fields and forests lost many a sone and flower, and one person noted over a hundred kinds of plants, similar to our native species. This same botanist, before reaching the Pacific coast, discovered a higher order of daisies, and it is confidentially believed that the characteristics and locality of this rare specimen were carefully noted.

The Red man was a curiosity to many of us, and we embraced every opportunity of familiarizing ourselves with his unique character.

One evening, on the Alkali plain, while our train was taking its usual rest, we enticed a young buck of magnificent physique, into our car. In a moment many of our charming ladies were gazing on, while the gentlemen were plying questions to our distinguished visitor. We pointed to one of our prettiest damsels, and asked the Indian if he did not want a squaw? He gave a characteristic shake of the head and said "no." "White woman!" "She's no workie!" "She's no washie." Thus showing his keen sense of his appreciation of the faults of the white race. It would not do to close our story without mentioning our favorite pastime. After the shades of night had fallen, the tables of the Pullman car were adjusted in the smoking room, and seated on opposing sides were our enthusiastic devotees of "Jenkins up." The shouts of the captains vied with the roar of the moving train and the snores of the old folks. Finally, dear readers, you know with me that our minds and hearts were often turned from the amusing instances of our trip to the more serious appreciation of this wonderful continent of ours, and the wisdom displayed in creating man and the universe. How often the words of the Psalmist were brought to our remembrance: "The Heavens declare the glory of God and the firmament showeth His handiwork!" Often our hearts were comforted by the sweet council of visiting ministers to our car, and the Christian fellowship of our own members made our journey a rare trip indeed. We were better men and women when the Golden Gate was reached, and we trust our wanderings helped prepare us to enter the pearly gates of the New Jerusalem.

Alcott, Anna J., Marlton.
Blakely, W. G., Camden.
Blakely, Mrs. W. G., Camden.
Bowman, Mrs. Myra J., Brooklyn.
Bowman, Miss, Brooklyn.
French, Ella, Moorestown.
Haines, Mrs. Emma, ———.
Harlow, Annie, Philadelphia.
Heaton, G. W., Moorestown.
Heaton, Mrs. G. W., Moorestown.
Nichols, Florence, Newark.
Overman, Prof. W. F., Moorestown.
Perkins, Almeda, Moorestown.
Pierce, George, Moorestown.
Putnam, Adelaide G., Newark.
Reynolds, Sarah, Moorestown.
Roubaud, Millard, Newark.
Shadler, Mrs. J. W., Moorestown.
Shoemaker, Mary, Bridgeton.
Shoemaker, Harriet, Bridgeton.
Sodden, Mrs., Newark.
Spawn, Eva, Newark.
Stimus, Clara, Moorestown.
Stimus, Howard, Moorestown.
Weis, Mrs. H., Newark.
Weis, Miss, Newark.
Wilson, Annie, Burlington.
Wilson, Mary, Burlington.
Wilson, Prof. L. M., Nyack, N. Y.

Burton.

In writing of the trip to California, let it be understood that the occupants of the car "Burton" had travelled but a few hundred miles when the goodfellowship and congeniality of the party, united us as one household, and we journeyed the remaining eight thousand miles as the "Burton family."

On our car there were thirty-seven persons—one a minister, three physicians, and fourteen were teachers.

The muse was early inspired to work, and we sang our song—to the tune of "Marching through Georgia"—in every car in our train. The first verse and chorus were composed by an estimable "Burton" lady, and verses were added by others.

After a few hours absence, to make a tour of some western city or village, and after our separation of several days, when we were scattered about in the different hotels of San Francisco, the refrain to this song would be the unfailing welcome on our return to the car.

The Christian Endeavor spirit strongly pervaded the Burton during the entire journey. We had some active workers with us, and scarcely a day passed without its service of song or Christian Endeavor prayer meeting. These meetings were usually held in the evening, and were conducted by different persons, notably Rev. Mr. Martine, Rev. Mr. Savage, Rev. Mr. Wyckoff and Dr. W. R. Ward. One evening the Rev. Mr. Ottman accepted an invitation to come into the "Burton" and give a Bible talk, and it was very interesting.

My impression is that these services worked much good, for in contemplating the works of God, whose wonderful creations were hourly entrancing us, we were all possessed of a spirit of profound adoration of Him who for our delight had made the snow-capped mountains, the matchless canons, the everlasting hills, which are but His footstools.

A pleasant feature of our journey was that of meeting old friends in some far western city.

Some of the Burton family met friends in San Francisco, and others had friends in Helena or Spokane or Minneapolis, and several met friends at Colorado Springs. These meetings and greetings and farewells will have a lasting effect on the impressionable mind.

Our experience in Yellowstone Park will probably be written in the general account of the trip, but we of the "Burton" would like to say of this "Wonderland of America," that it was a fitting climax to a wonderful journey. Every evening in the park a Christian Endeavor meeting was held at the hotel, where we would be stopping, and in each instance, but one, it was the first religious service that had ever been held on the premises. Let us hope that many have been held since, as a great number of Christian Endeavorers were following us.

The genial porter of the "Burton" rejoiced in the euphonious name of "Grenville Chalmers Davenport," and by common consent we called him "Chauncey M. Depew." For what reason I do not know, unless it was on the principle of the darkey who named his uncle January, because he was born in December.

When our journey was over we realized that our hats had been hanging on companion hooks so long that it seemed like "breaking home ties" to take them down for a final parting, but reunions of the Burton family have already been planned, and I am sure that friendships have been founded that will be lasting.

"THE BURTON SONG."

(*Tune—"Marching Through Georgia."*)

Here's to dear old "Burton,"
   The van car of the train,
All the way from Jersey shore
   She's led the sleeper chain.
Faithful still she speeds along
Toward the Golden Gate,
The brightest light from Jersey state.

CHORUS.

All hail! all hail! the Burton family,
All hail! all hail! we come from New Jersey!
Sisters we, and brothers strong,
We come from sea to sea,
Thus we sing the Burton greeting.

> A roll and coffee for two " bits,"
> A dish of "railroad frogs,"
> We glory in " conductor's punch,"
> We're bruised by many jogs,
> We've eaten " steam puffs" on the road,
> And snow balls on Pike's Peak,
> And slept while flying through the air.

When we separated from the New Jersey Special at Portland, and the Burton and the Saale were sent on to Yellowstone Park, the following verse was added:

> We come with hearty greeting
> From the Burton family,
> We've now annexed the sleeper Saale,
> We shout it joyfully.
> We're the two remaining families
> Of all the Jersey host
> Speeding to the National Park.

Ball, Hattie E., Newark.
Blauvelt, Annette, Newark.
Braaum, Sarah H., Newark.
Breck, Helen M., Brooklyn.
Burnite, Mary A., Newark.
Cuddeback, Olive, Paterson.
Doty, Jessie T., Lyons Farms.
Drake, Walter, Newark.
Drake, Mrs. Walter, Newark.
Edwards, Harriet S., Newark.
Eunson, Sarah A., Newark.
Farmer, Mary M., Newark.
Foster, Frank A., Newark.
Foster, Emma C., Newark.
Gasser, Louise J., Irvington.
Gauch, Lizzie E., Newark.
Goble, Etta R., Newark.
Henderson, Annie, Newark.
Hill, Bena, Newark.
Hill, Augusta, Newark.
Howell, M. D., Ella Woodward, Orange.
Mac Crellish, William A., Trenton.
Morris, Laura B., Newark.
North, F. A., Toms River.
Peer, E. Jane, Newark.
Pelser, Agnes E., Paterson,
Romain, Mary E., Newark.
Runyon, J. D., Newark.
Runyon, Mrs. J. D., Newark.
Savage, Rev. Charles A., Orange.
Schmidt, Christian, Newark.
Smith, Mrs. Fannie W., Newark.
Smith, Leona C., Newark.
Sweasy, M. Augusta, Newark.
Van Horn, M. D., Caroline H., Phila.
Ward, Mary C., Lyons Farms.
Ward, M. D., William R., Lyons Farms.

Utrecht.

Whatever may be said in this book of the other cars which composed our train, it is to be hoped that no one will imagine for an instant that any of them could compare favorably in any particular with the Utrecht. The reader will probably be told of the theological wisdom contained in the Superb, the youth and beauty in the Hebrides, the musical ability in the Sydenham, the literary genius in the Nadura, and so on through the long list, but all these were combined in our car, and to these accomplishments can be added a cordial geniality, and a regard for the comforts of one another, which will leave a delightful recollection as long as memory shall last.

There were doctors of medicine, doctors of divinity, doctors of dental surgery, doctors of law, and horse doctors on the train, but not one of them could compare with our Dr. Slack. You need not take my word for it, but ask any one who went with the excursion. They may first tell you that he found fault with Pike's Peak, because it was not high enough; with the Garden of the Gods, because there were no turnips planted there; with the railroad restaurants, because they gave him ham sandwiches instead of cheese; with San Francisco, because it was too cold; with Kansas City, because it was too hot, and with Yellowstone National Park, because the water in the hot springs was not hot enough; but ask them who attended to their headaches, backaches, earaches, toothaches and stomachaches, and who took the cinders out of their eyes, and they will tell you with one accord—Dr. Slack. With such medical talent, it was, of course, necessary that we should have a professional nurse, and we had one who was an adept at administering the doctor's very pleasant (?) potions, and whose soothing touch was as soft as velvet. During the day she tripped through the car as happy as a lark; but alas, when night fell, her happiness was at an end; for being as round as the proverbial dumpling, it was necessary for her to be tightly strapped to her berth to prevent her falling from it, which we all feared might wreck the car and train.

In section number one, was a young Somerville lawyer who made a great deal of noise, and who promised to be the protector of every one in the car should it be attacked by Indians, cowboys or robbers, but his bravery vanished in Helena, when a common, ordinary trolley motorman, without feathers, paint or lariat, offered to spoil his complexion if he ever dared call him Dennis again, and nothing more was heard of him during the remainder of the trip, and it has even been rumored that he was so crest fallen at his loss of reputation, that he decided not to come East, and left the party at Chicago.

Cox-ey's Army joined the party at Philadelphia. It was'nt a real army, you know; it only sounded so. It was composed of "Sis" and Cox-ey himself, in the first place, but was reinforced by a Shinn-dy from Ocean county, and his better half. After this, it needed no further additions to make section No. 3 the noisiest on the train.

The inmates of our car may not know that there were two occupants in section No. 1, but there were. A young jeweler occupied a berth there from eleven o'clock at night until six the next morning. The remainder of his time was spent in the Proteus. Strange, too, for the girls in our car were just as attractive as in any.

The most envied young lady on the train was from Trenton, and occupied section No. 2. The cause of this envious feeling was the free use of the telegraph wires from any point along the line, provided the message was sent to

NEW JERSEY TO CALIFORNIA, '97.

Trenton; and, of course, she had no desire to send one elsewhere. All the other girls wished their best fellows were managers of Western Union Telegraph offices.

The writer would like to distinguish everyone in the car, and would have no difficulty in assigning a specialty, to each, would space permit it, but as space is limited, he will close this letter by hoping that everyone enjoyed the trip and the companionship of the other occupants of the Utrecht, as much as he.

Bodine, J. P., Flemington.
Bolton, Rev. James, Roycefield.
Branigan, James Dunlap, Newton.
Clarke, Margaret P., Hackensack.
Cox, William E., Cream Ridge.
Cox, Mrs. William E., Cream Ridge.
Dungan, Nelson Y., Somerville.
Easton, F. C., Princeton.
Easton, Mrs. F. C., Princeton.
Erler, E. E., Newark.
Fell, Mrs. C. D., Glen Ridge.
Fulton, Joseph F., South Amboy.
Hanks, A. A., Jersey City.
Hendricks, Charles O., Newark.
Hibbs, Susan, Trenton.
Hibbs, Elizabeth L., Trenton.
Hill, F. Blanche, Andover.
Hill, Ida M., Andover.
Honness, B. F., Clinton.
Honness, Mrs. B. F., Clinton.
Ketcham, E. S., Newark.
Killinger, Pauline, Camden.
Lauer, Jr., John C., Newark.
Littell, Bloomfield, Orange.
Littell, Jennie, Orange.
McMurtrie, Mrs. George, N. Y. City.
Moore, Emma E., N. Y. City.
Munn, Grace A., Boonton.
Nevius, A. G., Flemington.
Petty, Edward L., Dover.
Roberts, Joseph Y., N. Y. City.
Rowland, R. M., Dayton.
Schlect, Mary, Haddonfield.
Shinn, George L., Haddonfield.
Shinn, Mrs. George M., Haddonfield.
Slack, M.D.,Clarence M., N. Brunswick.
Westervelt, Harry F., Newark.
Wilson, S. H., Andover.
Wilson, Mrs. S. H., Andover.
Zimmerman, H. B., New Brunswick.

Epsom.

The New Jersey C. E. Special for San Francisco, July 7-12, 1897, will live long in the memory of those who were among the tourists. And yet memory itself will rejoice in a souvenir that gathers up and records facts or incidents of that delightful journey. In our Pullman car, "Epsom," we had, as we went out, nineteen men and twenty-six women. The number was composed of farmers, business men and women. Students, three school principals, one professor of a classical academy, and four clergymen. Of course, there were besides, persons of leisure, or with occupations unclassified, who yet are most important members of society, as they were of this company. We met as strangers; we parted as friends, deeply interested in each other. The friendships one forms, even when we may not meet again, constitute one of the great benefits as well as charms of travel.

Our journey, beginning on the 28th of June, and ending on the 23d of July, was one of great pleasure. For this we owe not a little to our managers; very much to the faithfulness of the railroad employees, and more than we can tell to the kind Father of us all, whose protecting care kept us in safety in our outgoing and our incoming. One of our number is over eighty years of age, and his wife is nearly as old; a cheerful, goodly couple, who evidently enjoyed the journey from beginning to end.

One of our number, Mrs. Kane, was laid prostrate in San Francisco by some spinal difficulty, or paralysis. She was helped to the car for the homeward journey by her friends. Though constantly confined to her berth, she was a pattern of patience, cheerfulness and hope, from ocean to ocean. Though in privation and suffering, she evidently had "sunshine in her soul." And this had its full counterpart in the "sunshine" of care and kindness from Mr. and Mrs. Baker, who ministered to her every want. Nor do we forget the kind and much prized visits made to all who had need, by the trains' physician, Dr. Slack. In like manner would we make grateful mention of the cheerful and very helpful service rendered by Miss Geissele, a trained nurse, who formed one of our number on our return.

NEW JERSEY TO CALIFORNIA, '97.

I am sure many who were weary as the shades of evening drew nigh, will often think of the willing service Apgar rendered, in making ready berths for the night. Albert, our porter, certainly had "sunshine" in his face, and was faithful and efficient. But even he could not prepare two berths at once. Hence the appreciation above mentioned.

We had in our car, as did the others, many, a service of song and hour of devotion. Clergymen and laymen alike took part in the services, which were uniformly times of delight and refreshing to us all.

The Pullman car, Epsom, became our home on wheels for the Christian Endeavor Convention in San Francisco. It was our sitting room and bed room and often our dining room from Paulus Hook to Golden Gate.

We were such a congenial company that with inevitable annoyances, good nature predominated. There was sunshine in our souls whatever the external circumstances. Some found pleasant entertainment in our names. A lady said the "Epsom was a good car to be in when you are sick." I often heard it said to one of our number, "Why cough?" Although W. was fat and hearty. Bruin and Fox were not caged, but prudently located at the extreme of the car. Deer heads, jack rabbits and buffalo horns were only souvenirs. Our butcher had his pleasantest smiles for Mrs. Bull and Miss Bullock. The name of our tallest man was seldom dissociated from the mountain discovered by Pike. The Miller ground no corn that did get under his heels. The Bakers bought their bread as well as the rest of us. The Barber was charming, and yet the gentlemen would shave themselves and draw blood rather than adopt the Chicago idea. When a celibate preacher became rheumatic, he readily accepted the services of our young lady physician.

And this was not done because the regular doctor was Slack.

We shared "our mutual woes" and blessings. In a few things only was the shaving business overdone. When a good brother was crowded out of his own quarters by the ladies, I took him in. Then he took in my lunch and went into my grip and general belongings with strange disregard of muem et tunm. Once I had provided some delicious chicken for my time of need, perhaps on a side track in some barren spot, and simply saying "I'll pay you for this," he devoured it with all the sang froid of a Monmouth county mosquito. This was my return for folding him in my arms and holding him face down upon my lap, while a left handed preacher sewed a very important button on "his only pair." But with all his faults, I love him still.

At Salt Lake somebody gave our porter some fresh cherries. Porter soon became weaker than water. At bed time he was done up and thirty-six beds were not. The women could not make these beds, and in this emergency some of the men were women. But a farmer, a teacher and a preacher came to the rescue. At low twelve there were no "scenes of confusion, nor creature complaints." The porter was doubled up, but the passengers were extended at full length wherever the berth permitted.

"Still o'er these scenes will memory wake." The friendships formed on the Epsom will be lasting.

Apgar, Henry, Lebanon.
Baker, H. C., Jersey City.
Baker, Mrs. H. C., Jersey City.
Baker, Florence, Jersey City.
Baldwin, J. M., Newark.
Barber, Caroline A., Plainfield.
Bissell, W. E., Newark.
Bissell, Mrs. W. E., Newark.
Bruno, A. J., Newark.

Bull, Mrs. R. H., Newark.
Bullock, Noel J., Plainfield.
Conner, Prof. John G., Colora, Md.
Conner, Mrs. John G., Colora, Md.
De Mott, Bessie, South Amboy.
Doremus, Mrs. A. L., Jersey City.
Emson, Mrs. Sarah E., New Egypt.
Emson, Hannah A., New Egypt.
Foster, Mrs. A., Jersey City.

Fox, J. F., Annandale.
Frazee, Amanda M., Rahway.
Gasser, Louise J., Irvington.
Groendyke, J. N., Lebanon.
Groendyke, Mrs. J. N., Lebanon.
Ingalls, Charles L., Verona.
Jackson, Mrs. C. H., Rahway.
Kane, Mrs. H. S., Jersey City.
Kugler, Rev. J. B., Reaville.
Kugler, Mrs. J. B., Reaville.
Loizeaux, A. S., Plainfield.
Mershon, Rev. A. L., Annandale.
Mershon, Mrs. A. L., Annandale.

Mackenzie, Mrs. Duncan, Trenton.
Mackenzie, Margaret, Trenton.
Miller, O. P., Newark.
Peake, Rev. A. P., East Millstone.
Roberts, Leander, Plainfield.
Roberts, Mrs. Leander, Plainfield.
Stires, M. F., Jersey City.
Straub, Gottlob, South Amboy.
Sutphen, Mrs. M. C., Annandale.
Thayer, L. Elma, Plainfield.
Todd, Ada E., Annandale.
Williams, Samuel, Newark.

Proteus.

With one or two exceptions the excursionists from Paterson and vicinity occupied the Proteus. On the homeward trip the writer of these lines composed the following rhymes which were sung by the choir, which he organized in the car. Inasmuch as they were intended to review the period of time spent on the Proteus, they are inserted here after slight changes:

I. THE CAR.

(Tune—"Ta-ra-ra-boom-de-ay.")

Some travellers took a journey far,
They all rode in a Pullman car.
And nothing came their joy to mar,
For all went smooth without a jar,
    Yes they saw the great Pacific,
    And California with fruits prolific,
    Oregon and Washington,
    And back again to Paterson.

They rode out there on Proteus,
She ran just like an omnibus,
Her wheels were round, her berths were square,
But she made sure to get them there.
> O Proteus, but you were good,
> O Proteus, your floors are wood.
> A nice new carpet on your floor
> And silver handles on your door.

The porter said his name was Dave,
We made him work just like a slave,
Brushing clothes and making beds,
Finding combs for frowsy heads.
> He made us go to bed at eight.
> He would not let us stay in late.
> He thought he owned the train and us,
> But kept us straight without a fuss.

The conductor was a gentleman,
As cool and calm as a palm leaf fan,
His clothes were neat, his linen clean,
His buttons bright with glorious sheen.
> We'll remember him forever more,
> We'll think of him when life is o'er;
> We'll always praise the conductor
> Who took us to the Western shore.

No. II. THE PEOPLE.

(Tune—"Home, Sweet Home.")

Mid pleasures in palace cars, though we may roam,
From Paterson to Frisco, there's no place like home.
With rumbling and grumbling the train rolled along,
But all were heard singing the joyous old song.

Home, home, sweet, sweet home,
There's no place like home.

We had Ryle, Miller, Thompson and Quackenbush and Stiles,
Piaget, Hough and Duryee, and Schaub with many smiles.
Then Cuddeback and Belcher, and Beveridge alone,
Whose sister would have been there if she hadn't stayed at home.
  Home, home, sweet, sweet home,
  There's no place like home.

Then Tompkins and Mitchell and Spreen were in the van,
And Donkersley and Doremus who are a kind of a clan,
The Fowlers from Passaic, (and one had eyes that shone
When letters came in bunches from England's sunny home.)
  Home, home, sweet, sweet home,
  There's no place like home.

Miss Pelser, Miss Murray, Roy Hartley, Bess Van Winkle
She tackled the foot ball player and downed him in a twinkle,
And there was Mrs. Mathews who travelled all alone,
She never sneezed nor murmured, nor even wished for home.
  Home, home, sweet, sweet, home,
  There's no place like home.

When the porter began to make up the beds,
And people sat waiting with aches in their heads,
When the way to the berths had politely been shown,
T'was then with weary bones they began to wish for home.
  Home, home, sweet, sweet, home,
  There's no place like home.

When cinders were flying which made the faces black,
And everybody trying to get their baggage back,
When bathtubs were longed for in lands where unknown,
Then slimy, grimy travellers began to wish for home.
    Home, home, sweet, sweet home,
    There's no place like home.

Fried oysters and beefsteak and turkey and peas,
And many sweetmeats that appetites appease,
Clean dishes and table clothes and finger bowls alone,
And other things we had not, these we could get at home.
    Home, home, sweet, sweet home,
    There's no place like home.

We're glad that we looked at the wild and woolly West,
Which was supremely superfine when it was at its best.
But of all the fine places we've ever seen or known,
There's no place like home, there's no place like home.
    Home, home, sweet, sweet home,
    There's no place like home.

Beveridge, Bruce, Paterson.
Belcher, Mrs. William H., Paterson.
Doremus, Miss F. F., Preakness.
Doremus, Miss M. S., Preakness.
Donkersley, Mrs. H. S., Paterson.
Duryee, Rev. Abram, Cherry Hill.
Fowler, C. H., Passaic.
Fowler, Mrs. C. H., Passaic.
Fowler, Fannie A., Passaic.
Fowler, Irmah, Passaic.
Hartley, Roy, Paterson.
Hough, Thomas, Paterson.
Hough, Mrs. Thomas, Paterson.
Labar, A. I., Bangor, Pa.
Miller, John. New York.
Mathews, Mrs. M. E., Paterson.
Mitchell, Myra, Preakness.
Murray, Florence, Paterson.
Piaget, Alfred, Paterson.
Piaget, Mrs. Alfred, Paterson.
Quackenbush, William D., Paterson.
Ryle, Mrs. Nora, Paterson.
Ryle, Minnie, Paterson.
Spreen, Henrietta, Paterson.
Schaub, Henry, Jr., Paterson.
Stiles, Ezra M., Paterson.
Stiles, Mrs. Ezra M., Paterson.
Stiles, Miss Helen, Paterson.
Stiles, Mary, Paterson.
Stiles, Margaret, Paterson.
Stiles, Beveridge, Paterson.
Thompson, Rev. E. W., Paterson.
Tompkins, Miss Bertha, Paterson.
Van Winkle, Bessie, Passaic.

Keystone.

The car Keystone, as its name would indicate, was the most significant car on the New Jersey Special. Not a passenger on this car who will not fully and heartily endorse this statement. The name "Keystone" (and there is much in a name) means something. There were other cars on our Special that had names that seemingly were entirely meaningless. Perhaps the one who christened the cars with such names as the "Saale," "Proteus," "Burton," "Nadura," could tell us that these names are significant, and have a meaning. But to the average passenger they were names, and only names. There was the car "Hebrides," devoted exclusively to the use of the ladies, who preferred to be separated from the male passengers. In their female loneliness they began the study of the name of the car in which they were housed in their trip across the continent. They associated the name "Hebrides" with names in history and names in fiction. In fact they exhaust their knowledge of history and geography, and fail to see that a group of islands on the coast of Scotland should transfer their name to a car that is speeding its way across the great plains of the United States. Finally in their desperation, this car, into which not a man pillowed his head, except the porter, is called the "He-brides." The car "Epcom" was suggestive. In fact too suggestive. Not to mention the names of other cars, which, perhaps, others will do. We hasten to say that the only car that had a real significant name, a name that means something, was the car "Keystone." We all know the importance of the Keystone in the arch. It is that which binds the whole arch. Without it the arch would not be able to hold even its own weight. But with it, the arch becomes capable of supporting whatever may rest upon it. Now the car "Keystone," either because of its name, or some unexplained cause, was in point of position the most significant car on the New Jersey Special. Its place in the second section was about midway of the train. Thus like the Keystone in the arch it held the train together. When we became one section on our return trip, the "Keystone" was the connecting link between that which was known as the first and second sections, and in one or two instance when the train was reversed it was the car next the engine, and so came to occupy a very important position, for by its sturdy grip on the panting locomotive, it drew the entire train. But the car "Keystone" was a famous car on that New Jersey Special, not because of its name, nor of the position it occupied, but because of the occupants of this car. No more congenial spirits ever dwelt together than those who travelled for nine days and nights to reach the Golden Gate. Youth and old age found in each other delightful companionship. Wit, wisdom, scholarship, originality, beauty, refinement, in fact everything that could contribute to the delight of the soul, was to be found in the car "Keystone." The truth is, the car Keystone, and it might as well be spoken, had attractions for even outsiders. For twice was one of our fair passengers relieved of her pocketbook. And we suspect there were some who even lost their hearts. Should the youngest passenger, who was about twelve, live to be fourscore years, we believe he will cherish to the end of his days the fondest recollections of the noble car "Keystone."

When the train was nearing its destination at Oakland, Cal., one of the party on the car wrote the following:

FAREWELL TO THE KEYSTONE.

There is a car upon our train,
And there for nine days has remained.

And now a change we hope to make
And bide a wee at the Golden Gate.
Fare thee well! Keystone, we leave thee,
Do not let the parting grieve thee,
For the friendship we have formed
Will long remain, remain.

Adieu! adieu! Keystone, adieu!
We can no longer stay with you.
But in our hearts a place will save
For thee and friends that we have made.
We're glad to leave the desert drear,
And all the ills we had to fear,
And now our journey's almost o'er,
We soon shall reach the golden shore.

Beekman, Mrs. Sarah G., St. Johnsville, N. Y.
Case, Mr., Philadelphia.
Corfield, George H., Jersey City.
Corfield, Mrs. George H., Jersey City.
Conselman, Mrs. J. D., N. Y. City.
Conselman, Theo., N. Y. City.
Craft, Mrs. E. S., Washington.
Davenport, Mrs. Thos., Bound Brook.
Davis, Rev. W. E., Lebanon.
Dillman, Augusta, Mahanoy City, Pa.
Groff, Mary, Fort Plain, N. Y.
Higgins, Leila M., Flemington.
Jeffreys, Mrs. O., Washington.
Kelley, Myles, West Creek.
Leavitt, Mrs. C. B., Trenton.
Martine, Rev. A. I., Dunellen.
Moore, J. C., Elizabeth.
McClellan, D. Y., West Hoboken.
McGuire, M. Elizabeth, Ewingville.
Osborne, Lemuel, N. Y. City.
Patterson, Henry, Plainfield.
Phillips, James, Pennington.
Phillips, Mrs. James, Pennington.
Powelson, Edwin, Bound Brook.
Stall, Augusta, Pottsville, Pa.
Shields, Kate M., Washington.
Smith, K. Maud, Mahanoy City, Pa.
Seymour, Mrs. James M., Newark.
Wagner, Hattie, Mahanoy City, Pa.
Wilcox, Carra, Erskine.
Wilcox, Mrs. S. E., Erskine.

Dorante.

It has been impossible to get any sketch of this car. The reason cannot be lack of ability. For no car on the train had more literary talent. Those who were asked to contribute may have thought it better to "live in deeds and not in words."

The names of those who went to San Francisco on this car are given, as they have been gathered from many unauthentic sources, and therefore, probably, with many errors.

Baldwin, Louise A., Newark.
Baldwin, Lillian M., Newark.
Britton, Helen S., Trenton.
Busby, Dr., Camden.
Doremus, W. L., Montclair.
Danges, M. D., C. B., Camden.
Dutcher, Etta, Newark.
Hammond, Anna G., ——.
Harrison, Harriet, Newark.
Idell, Mrs. J. B., Brooklyn.
Johnson, Mrs. W., Newton.
Johnson, Miss L., Newton.
Lucey, Margaret, Jersey City.
Loring, J. C., ——.
Mac Call, Christine S., Newark.
Myer, Eva, Newark.
Osborn, Miss, N. Y. City.
Perry, Jennie, Brooklyn.
Perry, Nellie, Brooklyn.
Price, Lizzie, Elizabeth.
Price, Nellie, Elizabeth.
Parsons, Adaline, Plainfield.
Reese, Amanda, Phillipsburg.
Robinson, Mary, Plainfield.
Sloane, Mrs. G. W., Brooklyn.
Sloane, Miss M., Brooklyn.
Spencer, Mabel, ——.
Spencer, Mary, ——.
Schenck, Nellie, Holmdel.
White, Florence D., Jersey City.

New Hampshire.

The "New Hampshire" being the last car of the second section of the New Jersey "Special," and though a "Pullman," yet not being vestibuled (?) and thus having a clear platform from which a fine view could be enjoyed, was very popular. Indeed there was danger lest the occupants of the car should be crowded out of their rights by those from the cars ahead. "Jacob," the porter, however, proved to be equal to the occasion, and kept said back platform reasonably clear for the use of his own passengers. Our porter also showed great honesty in handing a roll of bills that he picked up upon the floor to the conductor, so that it was restored to its rightful owner.

When the second section became the first, as was the case beyond Kansas City, we came near being run into by that which had formerly been ahead of us, in a snow shed with a curve in it. This was owing to "criminal negligence" (so said an official) on the part of a brakeman, but fortunately the catastrophe was averted just in time!

Divine service was held aboard the car on Sabbath afternoon, July 4th. Rev. Archibald A. Murphy, of New Brunswick, N. J., preached from St. Mark 6:31: "Come ye yourselves apart into a desert place, and rest awhile." A text, the first part of which was thought to be applicable to the country through which we were passing at the time. The Rev. J. DeHart Bruen, of Union Seminary, assisted in the service. On the same "Independence Day" the passengers of the car were appropriately decorated with red, white and blue ribbon, thoughtfully brought along by a lady from New York city.

On the last day aboard, a mock marriage was celebrated. The bride was one of the young men dressed as a girl, and the groom came out of one of the cars ahead. A jolly girl from Hoboken acted as bridesmaid, and Jacob, the porter, was groomsman. Instead of a blessing, the officiating clergyman gave the couple a sound drubbing over the shoulders, and drove them from the car!

Bruen, H. N., Belvidere.
Bruen, J. H., Belvidere.
Carney, Elizabeth, ———.
Crowdis, Edwin G., Princeton.
Eick, J. H., Newark.
Emery, Mrs. E., Somerville.
Gilbert, Analita, Brooklyn.
Growenwoldt, Bertha, Hoboken.
James, Abbie H., Plainfield.
Kemp, Eva, Mt. Airy.
Kemp, Nellie, Mt. Airy.
Lee, Nina M., Trenton.
Loach, Minnie E., Elizabeth.
Lyle, William, Hoboken.
McGown, Miss B., Jersey City.
Murphy, Rev. A. A., New Brunswick.
Reed, M. D., Louis, Somerville.
Reed, Mrs. A. E., Somerville.
Rohn, Mrs. Helen M., Raritan.
Rudolph, H., Newark.
Rudolph, Mrs. H., Newark.
Savage, Rev. C. A., Orange.
Smith, Seymour L., Brooklyn.
Wheeler, Miss I. H., Jersey City.
Witt, Mrs. C. H., Hoboken.
Wyckoff, Mary, Bedminster.

The following poem was written by one of the ladies in Nadura:

BATTLE OF THE HE-BRIDES.

In torrents rain was falling,
    As darksome grew the night,
A band of lusty warriors
    Went forth unto the fight.

Full well they knew the danger
    That lurked in yonder car,
With crafty He-brides waiting
    And watching from afar.

Nor courage lacked they, truly;
    They nerved them for the fray,
And boldly stormed the entrance
    And forced the passage way.

Then up those He-brides rising,
    With fury in their eye,
With Amazonian courage,
    Resolved to win or die.

O, fiercely flew the pillows
    And smote th' encroaching band,
While shrill arose the war cry
    Far o'er the distant land.

The porter from above them
    Rained down his blows amain,
But up arose the warriors
    And hit him back again.

They pummeled Mr. Fitzer
    Until he lost his specs,
While Sinkinson and Terhune
    Were quite reduced to wrecks.

While Kaighn and Graff, the active,
    Bold Watermelon tall,
Dalrymple, Robinson and Cook,
    Though t they were at foot ball.

They fought until the shadows
 Had settled o'er the hill,
Then, with two female captives,
 Retreated, fighting still.

The He-brides, still undaunted,
 Exulting waved aloft
The hats and caps they'd taken,
 And at the Warriors scoffed.

"Oh, send for us our porter!"
 The captive maidens sighed.
"They'll bury a coon to-morrow,
 If he comes," the men replied.

Then Warne, the great peacemaker,
 He of the soothing tone,
Did strive to reconcile them,
 All single and alone.

The war of words that followed—
 We will not picture that.
At length th' exchange was finished—
 A maiden for a hat.

Then Peace, her wings extending,
 Outstretched o'er both the sides,
Forgotten was the battle—
 Nadura and He-brides.

Christian Endeavor song. Composed on board New Jersey Special, en route to San Francisco, '97:

CHRISTIAN ENDEAVOR SONG.

Tune—"Bringing in the Sheaves."

We're Endeavorers from New Jersey
Workers for the Master,
Heeding not the perils

Nor hardships on the way,
Looking unto Jesus,
Who encamped about us,
We went marching forward
Toward the Golden Gate.

[*Repeat last two lines for chorus.*]

Journeying o'er the desert,
On the rolling prairie,
Over Father of Waters
Toward the Golden Gate.
Through the mountain gorges,
In the depths of canons,
Sunset found us nearer
To the Golden Gate.

Now by snow-capped mountain,
Then by rushing torrent
Still our way we wended
Toward the Golden Gate.
Trusting still in Jesus,
Who had led us forward,
We kept pressing onward
Toward the Golden Gate.

At last we reached the waters
Of the peaceful ocean,
And bathed our weary feet
Within its cooling waves.
We journeyed from the East-land
Until we reached the west-land,
And then our journey ended,—
At the Golden Gate.

Still a longer journey
We're taking with the Master,
From these earthly sufferings
To a home beyond the skies.
Though oft we tread the thorn-paths

We'll follow in His footsteps,—
Soon we'll share His glory
Within the Golden Gate.

The ladies of the Hebrides for their own amusement, and to preserve a record of the startling events that transpired in their car on the night of July 16, issued a paper called the "Hebrides Herald." A copy was sent to the passengers of the Sydenham and the Nadura, their nearest neighbors. We insert some of the articles of the "Herald" and the resolutions adopted by the Sydenhamites:

Hebrides Herald.

JULY 7, 1897.

A RAID UPON THE HEBRIDES.

Bad, Bold Men Invade the Car—The Occupants Boldly Defended Themselves—Loss of Blood and Property on Both Sides—Two of the He-Brides Captured—They Languish for a Long Time Among the Raiders, but are Finally Restored.

To-day we send out our first issue of the "Hebrides Herald," and we bespeak for it a hearty patronage. So many startling events have followed each other in such rapid succession that out of the philanthropic spirit which prevails in the Hebrides was conceived the idea of preserving to this train and the world a record of them.

We feel sure that if one copy be read orders will come in thick and fast. Our talent is of the highest order and a rare treat is before you.

About 9 o'clock last evening the He-brides was visited by a very fine minstrel troupe led by Mr. Davis.

They rendered several pieces, all of which were very plaintive and effective in the extreme. All the He-brides were dissolved in tears, and the wailings which mingled with the strains of music were truly heartrending.

The occupants of the car showed their appreciation of the fine entertainment, throwing bouquets and a handsome remunerative collection in a hat.

THE FIRST CHAPTER OF THE BOOK OF THE CHRONICLES OF THE HEBRIDES.

Now it came to pass in the days of William the chief ruler, that some of the sons and daughters of the East said one to another. Let us go far away even to the land of Gold and hold a Convention in the name of those with whom we are associated. And because there were numbers in the land of Jersey who were so inclined they said, we will go with them. And Titus and Daniel and others said we will prepare the way before them:

And they departed from the city of Gotham on the eighth and twentieth day of the sixth month.

And many joined them on their way. And there were others to lead them, but Titus was chief. And they had with them one Edward named Theophilus of the family of Simmions who so conducted them on their journey that he greatly endeared himself to all.

And when they came to the great city whither they went, many received them courteously.

And others came from the East and from the West, from the North and from the South and convened with them.

And when the days were fulfilled they said: we will return to the land of our home and of our nativity. And they did so.

Now it was at the beginning that because there were among the Jerseyites many widows and maidens, Titus said: we will put them one by another, and they shall have none to molest or make them afraid, and he did so. Therefore were they called He-brides. But it came to pass on the eve of the sixteenth day of the seventh month, that the young men who were their neighbors, said, among themselves, we will go and see those with whom we have had friendly intercourse and see how they do.

So they came with great friendliness of manner.

But the maidens were startled and resisted them with weapons and with great vigor.

Then they said we will retreat with quietness and bravery. But they were assaulted more and more and their progress was obstructed, so that they could turn neither to the right hand or to the left.

And Edward the porter also fought valiantly for those whom he had in charge.

But Millie, the daughter of Lawrence, whose surname was Trimmer, and Lilla, the wife of Edwin, were taken in captive and remained in bondage.

But Daniel who was also called Ruby, who had warned us on our way, came with the flag of truce and peace was declared and the captives returned to their waiting companions.

NEW JERSEY TO CALIFORNIA, '97.

I. Man, car,
   Friday night,
   Great raid,
   Pillow fight.

II. He-brides,
    Great uproar,
    Take stand
    On the floor.

III. Men crawl
     On hands and knees.
     Pillows fly
     Thick as fleas.

IV. Caps lost,
    Glasses broken,
    Heels taken
    As a token.

V. Men pass
   By the Porter,
   Soon decide
   Not to loiter.

VI. Girl caught,
    Carried off,
    He-brides
    Only laugh.

VII. Man sent,
     Flag of truce,
     Much talk,
     No use.

VIII. Caps fixed,
      As a ransom,
      Such treatment,
      Very handsome.

IX. Peace declared.
    Treaty signed,
    He-brides
    Of one mind.

X. That when it's time
   To go to bed,
   Nadura wants lunch
   In the car ahead.

HE—BRIDES TO THE RESCUE.

They come! they come! a thousand strong,
With cannon's roar and clashing steel;
Arise! arise! in might and strength,
And with your prowess *do* the throng—
    He-brides to the rescue.

Each woman seize her *sabre white*,
And there her strong, right arm uplift;
Let each one see the blow's not SLIGHT—
Whack! slap! shout and clap—
    He-brides to the rescue.

Hark! from the enemy retreat is called,
And forth they go with saddened mien;
With battered hats and heads they go—
And in the fray there was many a fall—
    He-brides to the rescue.

Hurrah! the victory is yours—
Your *general* led you brave and true!
Death to him who at you sneers
While we are on this *best* of *tours*—
    Fair He-brides, you're Queen.

Advance, Oh men of Nadura
Strong, ran the battle cry,
But ere they reached the inner door
The pillows began to fly.

Then waged the war
Both fierce and long,
The girls all right,
The men all wrong.

Again the foe did gain the door,
Again were beaten back,
Two fair young captives gained
Were *meekly* handed back.

So ended all the fray,
Their lesson learned had they,
And the warriors of the Hebrides
Float a victorious banner to the breeze.

    I am asked to write a story
      Of the people on this train,
    We've funny folks and sunny folks,
      And pretty ones and plain.

    The first is our Conductor,
      A little man, and slow,
    And to everything we ask him
      He replies: "I do not know."

The next is Mr. Davis,
  His patience far excels
A noted man of ancient times
  Of whom the Bible tells.

Mr. Warne, on our committee,
  Is brave and true and bright;
He hastened to our rescue
  In the riot of last night.

And there is Mr. Dyott,
  So spiritual and good,
He is constantly dispensing
  Our heavenly drink and food.

The next is our good porter,
  He serves us night and day,
He is always kind and patient
  If we let him have his way.

And there are many others
  Whom I would like to name,
And give them honored mention
  Upon this roll of fame.

Their bright and sunny faces,
  Their words of kindly cheer,
Will linger in our memories
  For many a coming year.

But the train keeps moving onward,
  And we soon must say good bye,
God grant we all may gather
  At the Golden Gate on high.

SYDENHAM RESOLUTIONS.

Whereas, It hath seemed good unto the innocent maidens and still hopeful widows of the Hebrides to send unto their neighbors the exemplary, esteemed, honored, and illustrious Sydenhamites, an engrossed copy of their artistically illustrated, erudite, felicitous, voluminous and exhaustive paper, entitled "The Hebrides Herald" of July the 17th, A. D. 1897; and

Whereas, The contents of said paper revealed the sad calamity which befell the unsuspecting and unprotected inhabitants of the He-brides, upon the night of the 16th instant, when a band of midnight marauders, with malice aforethought and evil intent, made a fierce onslaught; and

Whereas, These defenseless females so valiantly resisted and ultimately routed the barbarians wih loss of blood, feathers, shoe heels, frizzes, pillow cases, physical energy, et cetera, sleep and so forth; and

Whereas, Two of the fairest flowers that bloom in the garden of the He-brides were rudely plucked by ruthless hands, and forced to droop and wither for a season in the pestilential atmosphere of their Nadurian prison; therefore, be it

Resolved, That the exemplary, esteemed, honored, and illustrious Sydenhamites do hereby express their profound appreciation of the merits of the artistically illustrated erudite, felicitous, voluminous and exhaustive paper, and their unfeigned gratitude; therefore, and be it further

Resolved, That they extend their sincere, heart searching, heart rending, overwhelming and all-sufficient sympathy to these harmless creatures for the indignities and irreparable loss which they sustained at the hands of the foe; and be it further

Resolved, That hearty congratulations be extended to the injured and innocent for their unprecedented achievements manifested in their complete annihilation of the enemy, and the restoration of their fair flowers to their Hebridesian paradise; and be it further

Resolved, That a copy of these resolutions be spread upon the minutes of the New Jersey Special, and placed in the archives of the New Jersey Historical Society, and that a copy be sent to the once suffering, but now triumphant Hebrides.

www.ingramcontent.com/pod-product-compliance
Lightning Source LLC
Chambersburg PA
CBHW030344170426
43202CB00010B/1236